# How to
# change the world with
# one pitch

*A blueprint for winning at life
one conversation at a time*

# Daniel Batten

How to
change the world with

# one pitch

National Library of New Zealand Cataloguing-in-Publication Data

Batten, Daniel.

How to change the world with one pitch

Published by Beyond the Ceiling Books

ISBN 978-0-473-39213-0

First published 2017

Ten percent of profits from this book go to the School of Unlimited
Learning, a new fund to finance an approach to education outlined
in Chapter 4: Conviction.

Designed by Jacinda Torrance, Verso Visual Communications

# How to
## change the world with
# one pitch

A blueprint for winning at life
one conversation at a time

Daniel Batten

BEYOND *the* CEILING

*Authentic Influence*

# Acknowledgments

To my first teacher, my mother Juliet Batten. The formula laid out in this book is powerful and brings together elements that have not been brought together before. This was only possible because of how she helped me from an early age to uncover patterns, ask good questions and be fascinated by language.

To my leadership coach, Shannon. You inspired me to see the potential that I did not at first see in myself, then guided me through the steps to realizing it.

To my wife, Su Yang. You have been the most supportive, loving, caring, patient and belief-filled wife a husband could wish for. Without your support, this book would have been impossible.

To my mindset coach, Sri Sri Ravishankar. Years ago, you gave me the confidence to start my first company, believe in myself, cultivate my intuition and dedicate my life to service. You have guided and supported my every step since.

# How to get the most from this book

**1. Treat your book as your training manual, not a library book**

The more you personalize this book, the better. Underline, highlight, scrawl in the margin – because this is a book you'll come back to again and again.

**2. Commit to read for implementation, not information**

I _____ (name)

commit on _____ (date)

to trying out the great ideas that I discover in this book, so that I and the world will benefit from them.

**3. Get support**

There's a group of people who will inspire and help you with Changing the World One Pitch at a Time. They're waiting for you to join right now at **fb.me/pitchtowin**. Just click the Like button to be part of this group.

# Contents

Pitching is the art and science of using language to influence outcomes.

# Preface

Is this book for you? The tools in it involve no spin and no manipulation. They have been shaped so they only work if your intention is to do something positive in the world through your leadership, products, services, ideas, creations or cause. If you want to spin and manipulate words for your own ends, if you do not have any vision for yourself or your business beyond profit, this is the wrong book for you.

So, who is it relevant to? This book is for people who want to change the world for the better. My clients have used the pitching principles covered in this book not only to win sales and investment pitches, but also to succeed in job interviews, secure a large promotion or pay rise, win grants or sponsorship – even when dating. In every case, they enjoyed a success rate of, or close to, 100 percent.

Pitching is a science. Because of that if you apply the formula outlined in this book, you *will* achieve abundance. That much is certain. In fact, it will happen more easily than you imagine. Because pitching is a science, you can learn the components of success easily. Through iterating, even an unsuccessful pitch will quickly become successful.

However, this is true only if you know the right elements of the pitch to focus on. These are the 16 elements in this book.

Saying that pitching is an important aspect of selling is like saying the sun is an important aspect of enjoying a summer holiday. True, but I can think of other problems the world would have if there were no sun, so it's an absurd understatement of its value.

So, what other problems would your world have if you weren't effectively pitching? In a world without pitching, you would experience at least one of these 10 problems:

1. Failing to change the world for the better.
2. Working on projects that go on too long, causing low energy and attrition.
3. Having long sales or negotiation cycles.
4. Working with disengaged, or inconsistently engaged, teams.
5. Achieving a low or inconsistent rate of winning bids or tenders.
6. Not getting investment with the right terms, people and time frame.
7. Failing to inspire others to change their attitudes or behavior.
8. Feeling like people don't value your voice or even recognize that you have a voice.
9. Knowing you are not (yet) the leader you have the potential to be.
10. Believing you will die with your dream inside you.

Pitching is *the* simplest, most direct and most effective way to solve these problems.

If you have experienced, and are likely to re-experience, even one of these problems in business or in life, applying the tools in this book will ensure you never experience that problem again.

What level of outcome can you expect from applying these tools? Let's take Number 5 from the list of problems above – having a low or inconsistent rate of winning bids or tenders. I chose that one because it's easy to measure.

By measuring win rates before and after I introduced clients to the tools in this book, I've found that the following occurs:

- a win rate of 20 percent will increase to around 80 percent
- a win rate of 50 percent will increase to around 90 percent
- a win rate of 90 percent will increase to around 98 percent.

The consistent rule seems to be that you will lose around four times less often. I believe the same is true for all 10 categories in the problem list. You will lose four times less often! Even the few clients who had never won a pitch, mostly won their next pitch by using the tools in this book. I expect the same even for someone who has spent 10 years getting nowhere – that they will win their next pitch using these tools.

The most important decision you make as a leader is to be the change you want to see in the world. Therefore, this book works on two levels. It is not only about pitching, it is a pitch.

At one level the book is pitching ideas, concepts and constructs. And at another level, it is also pitching why you should not just read these ideas, but apply the tools to your work, your life and your life's work. It therefore not only introduces you to ideas that will help you in your business and your life, it provides an example of how do what the book is about – how to pitch.

The fastest way to change the world for the better is to give good people great influence.

# Introduction

In a lifetime, you're lucky if you get to work in one team that takes a product global. In January 2007, having just handed over the reins to a new CEO at a company I'd co-founded, I was feeling fortunate to have worked in three.

In the next phase of my life, I was to fulfill a dream to help grow not just one company, but many. The first step in my new chapter was to reflect on and learn from where I'd been. That one reflection, 10 years ago, led to this book.

I asked myself a seemingly innocent question, "What caused us to win?"

I took out a single sheet of paper, and in just five minutes I scrawled down a list of seven actions. I paused five minutes, wrote an eighth action, then looked at the paper. I knew I now had the recipe for how we got to where we did.

I looked at that list a second time and realized that, while in a raw state, this was a blueprint for how *any* company could win.

I looked a third time and realized that, while in an even more raw state, this was a blueprint for influencing *any pivotal conversation in life*.

So, what was on that sheet of paper that has inspired me not only to help many entrepreneurs build many companies, but also to write a book?

There was one action that took a long time and involved hard work. It was "build a great product."

But the other seven actions took a short time and involved a key skill. Those seven items were all key conversations or presentations. They were all *pitches* of one form or another.

Those seven pitches were:

1. Deciding to continue after a failed first investment pitch.

2. Our successful first round of capital-raising.

3. The conversation that led to our first rock-star developer joining us.

4. Asking the first users of our product to recommend it to others.

5. The presentation that got us our first sale.

6. The message we wrote about our product that propelled us to be the number one download on Apple.com (the precursor to the app store).

7. Asking the right person to be CEO after I stepped down.

Looking again at the list, I realized that these pitches involved only five types of people. They were:

- an investor
- a customer
- a team member
- a partner or board member
- yourself (I'll talk more about this one later).

This led me to conclude that once you have a great product, your success is determined by having powerful conversations with the right person.

That means that once you have a great product, *your success is down to your pitch.*

No one had ever put it to me that bluntly. I was stunned by the conclusion I'd reached. Had I made a mistake? Was I oversimplifying things? My limiting belief at that time that things must be complex caused me to hide my conclusion for fear I'd be laughed at.

Everyone around me was talking about market validation, timing, IP protection, governance, measuring strong commercial markers, the ability to pivot fast, a lean methodology and process as the factors that caused business success. And yet two questions kept coming back to me:

"Didn't Henry Ford just pitch successfully to a team of people who joined his company and made things for him?"

"Weren't Steve Jobs' only two skills the ability to put together an innovative product and the ability to put together an innovative pitch?"

I started researching these people and others who'd built winning companies. The same conclusion kept getting reinforced. Yet still I doubted it could be this simple.

I decided I needed to test the idea further. I stopped doing traditional business coaching. I stopped having conversations with my clients about the complexities of growing a business and instead showed them how to do two things – *influence others* and *influence themselves*.

In other words, I showed them how to pitch. My method of working with them was itself a pitch. Rather than talk about what to do and how to do it, which is what I'd been taught to do as a coach, I pitched to them the value of changing their behaviors and beliefs.

I *pitched* to them why they should master *pitching*.

The impact was immediate. Suddenly results that had taken six months started happening in one. Encouraged, I simplified my approach further. Then results started occurring by the end of the first session. And these were not limited to business results.

After a single session, the approach of pitching – to others and themselves –has seen my clients:

- win their next pitch after losing their past three pitches
- increase their new business win rate from 21 percent to 87.5 percent
- achieve their commercial results for the year*
- give up smoking
- leave a destructive relationship
- increase their charge rate, leading to doubling their profitability

- aim to be a $1 billion company, not a $10 million company
- get paid twice as much for the work they do*
- get happily married and have children
- become a professional singer
- see a complete performance turnaround in a team or team member.*

*These outcomes occurred for many clients after just one session.*

More importantly, though, not only were the results deep and immediate, they were happening consistently. This level of result started happening in *every* person I coached.

That was the proof I needed. Finally, I had won the most important pitch of my life. I'd won over the most stubborn and difficult person I've ever pitched to – me!

After seven years, I'd finally accepted that business success could be described by a phrase that sounded like a clumsy marketing claim – easy and immediate.

Through sheer weight of evidence, I changed my mindset and overcame my limiting belief that obtaining business success must be long, stressful and complex, and involve many external factors coming together.

By using the tools in this book, none of your pitches need ever be as testing or as hard won as the pitch I finally won with myself.

You're now going to read some bold claims. You'll either be excited by them or skeptical, as I was. Either way it doesn't matter. If your intention is to allow this book to have a transformational impact on you, I suggest that you don't be too quick to agree or disagree with these claims. Instead, suspend both belief and disbelief and simply be curious to read on and see what supporting evidence is revealed.

A pitch is a powerful conversation with the right person.

# Key ideas in this book

1. Pitching is *the* most important skill in business.

2. Pitching is *the* most important life skill you have not yet learned.

3. This book synthesizes the four parts of pitching into one simple practical form so you can be successful in your quest to lead the world to a better future.

4. The tools in this book can be learned by any committed person, including you.

5. The 16 elements of the pitch in this book are *the* essential elements of pitching. Anything else you do is non-essential. But ignore any of these elements and you will cripple your chance of winning a pitch.

6. Pitching applies to every one of these elements of business and life:

   • having someone see the value in your idea

   • enrolling someone in a cause or course

   • having someone see you in a new light

   • having someone accept your recommendation or referral

   • taking a relationship to the next level.

7. The information age creates a weight of *information*. This creates many overwhelmed people getting underwhelming success. Pitching creates a counterweight called *influence*. This causes an in-flow of people getting an overflow of success.

I wrote this book based on the above seven claims with three higher intentions in mind:

1. To write a book that could change the world for the better by helping over 100,000 good people to gain great influence.

2. To use stories, metaphors, questions and framing to make it almost impossible for you *not* to implement what you read.

3. To include only the most useful, powerful and implementable strategies to reveal to you.

## How to implement this book

With such bold claims, you may be left wondering whether there are any circumstances under which these ideas do not work. The answer is that there are two, and I suggest you decide right now that you will *not* be in one of these two categories or put down the book immediately.

1. You have not made a commitment to yourself to change your behavior. While the ideas in this book are *simple*, they are not all *easy*. Some of them require a new level of courage from you. If you are not committed to exercising the courage it takes and expect that simply by being informed you can become successful, you will not become successful.

2. You are not interested in serving others. All the tools in the book work because they tap into a universal human need to serve others, and the universal human need in others to be cared for by you. If you only want to learn to pitch better so you can line your own pockets, and you couldn't care less about making positive change in the world while that happens, these tools will be rendered powerless in your hands.

If you are not in one of those two categories, I have a challenge for you before you read another page. I challenge you to make a pledge to yourself. It is the same pledge I make to myself when I read a book. Because of this pledge, I now read only one tenth the number of books, while receiving 10 times the benefit. I believe the same will be true for you when you make this pledge.

This pledge is, "I am reading for *implementation*, not *information*. Therefore, I will implement what I learn."

If it's your intention to read for intellectual understanding, no pledges are necessary. However, if it's your intention to gain an exceptional level of benefit for a small amount of reading, then the way to do that is to *commit right now to implement in the service of others what you learn from this book.*

If you haven't already, go back to the front of this book, and sign and date the pledge there.

## Why learn to pitch?

Learning to speak influentially is the one of most important things you can learn to do if you want to reach your potential.

Oratory and rhetoric were once taught at school. Their loss from the curriculum is also a loss to you. They are not only necessary skills, they are powerful ones. In writing this book, I'm handing this power back to you.

The truth is, unless we master telepathy, our words are *the* way we connect with each other. The person who cannot pitch can only use language to inform and entertain. Monkeys use language to inform and entertain. So, if you fail to learn to pitch, you are compromising your ability not only to reach *your* human potential but *the* human potential. That is why I believe pitching is the highest form of human expression.

Because of a lack of skill in pitching, most people die with unexpressed visions, unbuilt products, unwritten symphonies and unformed companies inside them.

I come across these people all the time. Dying with your dream inside you is one of the saddest fates I know, because it represents a life purpose not even explored, a wider community or global benefit not realized.

Dying with your dream inside you – or floundering outside you – is your certain fate if you don't know how to pitch.

## How do you learn to pitch?

There are two ways to learn how to pitch. The first is to separately master and synthesize the four elements of pitching. Here's the recipe for that path.

### Path A

*Mindset*

Spend years mastering how to pitch to yourself. Learn how to influence your own belief systems and clear your mind of doubts, so that at critical pivots in your life you will make the right decisions. Travel to the East to discover knowledge that is not part of the Western view of how to pitch.

*Tactics*

Get a coach who can reveal tactical elements of winning through words by using intelligent moves and countermoves not traditionally taught in the business world. Study the best performing sports teams of all time for the tactical maneuvers, training techniques and bold moves they use to get results.

*Delivery*

Learn stagecraft. Learn improvisation theatre for conversational pitches and formal theatre for presentational pitches. Study the use of the voice and read widely on body language. Get involved in theatre groups so you can practice these techniques.

*Message*

Become a linguist, and study narrative (story). Become an entrepreneur and give many pitches. Read everything there is on pitching. Learn the formulas. Learn how to message. Do some sales training. Do some marketing training. Learn the templates of how to pitch in your given form. Study the best pitchers of our time and the pitch decks of successful pitchers over the years.

Once you have completed these four stages, spend some time sifting through what is relevant and what is not, until you arrive at your own synthesis of a system for pitching.

**Path B**

Read this book.

## Philosophical basis to this book

There is a philosophical basis to this book. If you want to know the basis, study the philosophy of Bruce Lee. If you want to succeed in business and life, read this book.

Lee observed that over time, martial art forms, and indeed any system of thinking, gets stylized. The moment the martial art form gets stylized, it stops working in a street fight. He also observed that in a street fight, only four techniques were required – strike, trap, grapple and hold.

Lee went through every martial art form, learning it thoroughly and then throwing away anything that didn't work and keeping the few things that did. He created a combined form that he called "simple, brutal and direct."

But he didn't study only martial arts; he went further afield, studying javelin, for example, searching for a formula for "where power comes from." He did this because he was attached to his outcome, but ruthlessly unattached to how he got there. Because of that, he developed the most innovative and effective approach to martial arts known. It wasn't just a little bit more effective, it was exponentially more effective.

Lee threw out anything complex and retained only the things that would work on the street. He observed that learning a martial art under a skilled teacher doesn't take a lot of time – it just takes learning the *right* moves and getting good at a handful of simple, implementable techniques.

By mastering these techniques, Lee could hit so hard that an average fight lasted 11 seconds. By mastering these techniques Lee became undefeatable. By mastering these techniques, Lee taught others to become effective on the street in a short time.

Unlike the martial art, in the pitch art there is no fight. But there is a street on which you need to win. This street is the place where the decisions are made that affect whether or not you get the backing you need.

The martial artist influences the physiology of the fight, but the pitching artist influences *the psychology of the decision.*

If you want to learn pitching techniques that look impressive and feel good to your ego, there's plenty of content on how to do that. But if you want to learn a few moves that are *simple, bold and direct* to become effective on the street in a short time, read this book.

# A tale of two pitches

## Pitch A

On 3 September 2003, I lost in the streets. I didn't just lose, I was taken down badly. I tell this story in full in Chapter 3: Growth Mindset. The pitch was so bad that the best two comments I got that day were, "I'm surprised you're still standing" and "I like you, but I really didn't like your pitch."

I vowed after that experience I would never again be taken down like that. Because of that vow, nine months later, I gave a second pitch.

## Pitch B

On 4 May 2004, the pitch and the person giving it had changed so much that our high-tech company, Helix8 (not its real name), became the first in New Zealand to secure investment from an angel investment firm.

This result was covered in all the major business magazines and newspapers in the country. The pitch not only opened the door for our company, but provided the blueprint for how we would achieve future success. It also activated the high-tech angel investment scene in New Zealand.

Twelve years later, high tech is New Zealand's third largest export earner, and the signs are that it could become number one. The product we created, and the copycats it spawned, mean that 100,000 molecular biologists in universities and research institutes can do research twice as fast in fields that include breast cancer and malaria.

The reputation and experience gained from this success helped me get to work closely with five top high-tech CEOs over two years on all four elements of pitching. Their dedication to learning saw them secure more investment between them in half the time it took the largest angel investment group in the country to do so. They also achieved more than 337 percent sales growth and 619 percent profit growth, gained rock-star employees and incredible board members, and most of them are now on a trajectory to becoming $1 billion companies by valuation.

The world has changed for the better because of one pitch, in many unimaginable ways.

What made the difference between Pitch A and Pitch B? After all it was the same:

- company
- product
- level of progress
- opportunity
- level of market validation
- person giving the pitch.

So clearly it wasn't the product or opportunity that mattered. Clearly also, it wasn't the person who mattered either. Frankly, I pitched badly that day in early fall 2003 in San Diego. It wasn't the person, it was *what that person had learned*.

And as it turned out, what that person had learned, could be learned by *anyone*.

In those nine months that changed everything, I'd learned four powerful rules within each of four aspects of pitching:

- mindset
- tactics
- delivery
- message.

Four areas, each with four rules – 16 elements of pitching.

These 16 elements are the blueprint for how to change the world with one pitch. By reading this book, you will learn this blueprint and how to apply it.

When I listen to people pitch, I no longer hear words, I see them. I see a jigsaw puzzle that has a picture on it. That puzzle may be complete or incomplete. Sometimes, I see the right pieces but in the wrong order. Sometimes, I see some pieces are upside down, having the opposite of the intended effect. Sometimes I see missing pieces, and the missing piece may be a metaphor, a story, a small delivery flaw, a single statement or, in some cases, a single word.

# The 16 elements of influence

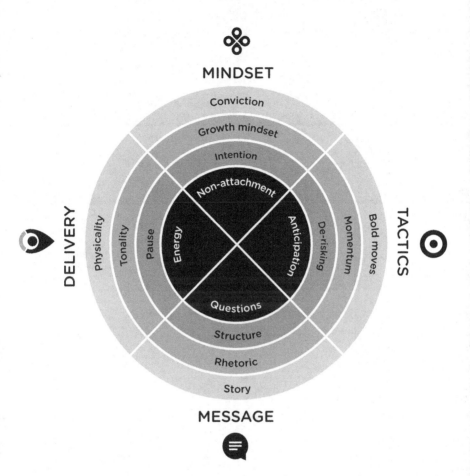

Fortunately, pitching is not a 1000-piece puzzle. It is only a 16-piece puzzle. To change the world, or your world, through your pitch, you need not *master* all 16 pieces. You only need to *apply* them.

In a pitch the feedback you get is binary. You either move ahead, or you don't. This book is the formula for making this binary outcome a 'yes' – almost every time you pitch.

MINDSET

When I help a client to win many pitches over time – as opposed to winning just one pitch – I always start with mindset.

Why? Because I've tried not starting with mindset and it doesn't work!

Learning skills without the right mindset is like planting seeds then preparing the soil – it's the wrong way around. It means you just hope the soil is fertile.

I never rely on hope and nor should you. Hope is the bastion of the person who doesn't believe in their own potential to influence outcomes. Hope says, "My success will ultimately be determined by *factors outside of me*." Hope is the opposite of self-responsibility.

So, just how powerful is mindset?

One company that was a client of mine was winning 20.5 percent of its pitches and proposals. I discussed with the CEO what the company needed and we agreed that my first intervention would be to spend one day with the people giving pitches and writing proposals and work with their mindset.

Six weeks later, the CEO called me and said, "We've won seven out of our last eight pitches." Two years later, their win rate remains above 81 percent. Needless to say, the difference between the two win rates was worth a lot of money to that company.

We achieved that change in one day. That's why mindset is the first section in this book.

So why is the right pitching mindset so powerful?

Without clear thinking, there can be no clear speaking. Without clear speaking, there can be no clear decision making from those you seek to influence. Simply put, everything starts with mindset.

One of the core reasons that many people who seek to influence others, such as salespeople or leaders, fail to do so is because they have the right tools but their mindset is in the wrong place.

Here's an example. Over the years, I've had many people approach me wanting assistance in gaining capital for their companies. At least half of these people had zero chance at gaining capital because of a fatally flawed belief that they had been unable to shed. What is this belief?

It is a belief that securing capital for their company could be solved by finding the right investor. In other words, they believed it was a problem of *finding* someone rather than them *becoming* the person investors want to be found by.

With this belief system, a person will fail again and again. They will continue again and again to blame the person they are pitching to for not seeing the obvious truth of their pitch. They will continue their flawed search for the perfect investor or the intelligent customer who gets it – that special person who has both intellect and vision.

This is a convenient zero-responsibility approach to life called prospect blame syndrome (PBS). PBS allows you to be bad at conveying the value of what you have and blame other people for not understanding you.

Fortunately, if you are one of the few who truly choose to take responsibility for your own powers of influence, your chances are high of becoming the person investors and customers want to be found by.

Ollie (names have been anonymized for privacy) was one entrepreneur who suffered from PBS. When I first met Ollie, he told me that investors lacked the vision to see the true potential of what he had. I told him directly that investors lacked nothing. I said, "It's you who lacks the potential to speak to them in their relevant language and have them get the power of your vision and the strength of your commercials."

At that moment, Ollie made a choice that changed history. He decided to listen to direct feedback that could grow him and his vision, as opposed to listen to his ego, which wanted to believe that he didn't need to change and that other people were the problem.

Because of that, Ollie and I could do some work on his pitch. Within one month Ollie's pitch had changed completely. Because of that, within one month he got his first piece of successful traction after 10 years of wandering in the wilderness. You can find out exactly how Ollie changed his pitch and how that pitch changed the world in Chapter 16: Story.

None of that work would have been possible if Ollie had not decided to change from a *blame mindset* to a *self-responsibility mindset*. We had to start on mindset first.

However, blame mindset is not the only obstacle. There are four mindset adjustments required, which you will read about in the next four chapters.

I was a late convert to the need to start with mindset. As a linguist, I couldn't wait to start talking about framing, story and ways to be direct yet friendly at the same time. But several years ago, an embarrassing experience changed all that.

I was running sales training for corporates at the time. I'd just got a job helping a team to sell their solution over the telephone. Because of the busy nature of their work and their schedule, the team could not take the normal two days out in a row for sales training. So, we divided the training in half, with a sales mindset day first then a sales skillset day two weeks later.

I was wholly unprepared for what happened. The mindset day went well. By the end of the day, people were happy and enthusiastic, as people often are after overcoming limiting beliefs that have stood in the way of them achieving their goals in business and life.

However, this caused a problem. When I arrived for the sales skillset day two weeks later, they were already doing almost everything I was about to train them to do! I was completely unprepared for the extent to which they had taken on the mindset principles we'd covered.

Because of their change in behavior, not only were they closing vastly more sales over the phone, selling higher volumes to each customer and taking less time to do it, their change in mindset had spilled into life outside work. Several people had taken up exercise, a woman had quit smoking and the general mood in the room was about 354 percent more positive than it had been two weeks earlier.

On one level I was so proud of them. I felt like telling them, "You don't need the stuff I was about to tell you. You're already doing it." It was a tough day as bit by bit we realized that I had little to add to what they had already started doing.

From that point forward, I cut in half the time I took to do sales training and just focused on sales mindset, plus a few skills targeted at where people most often fall down – to frame key elements of the sales process.

These one-day mindset-focused sale sessions continued to lead to some of the most significant and immediate turnarounds in sales performance I've seen.

Whether it's pitching for multimillion dollar investments or tele-sales, pitching to gain a rock-star employee, or as a leader pitching the benefits of behavior change to a member of your team, the rules of mindset in this section are universally applicable to every type of pitch you'll ever give.

For that reason, what I covered years ago with that tele-sales team closing contracts worth hundreds of dollars is the same as what I cover today with entrepreneurs pitching to government ministers where a win can be worth billions.

There are a lot of mindset adjustments that will matter little to the number of pitches you win. But there are four mindset adjustments that will make a big impact on how many pitches you win, and therefore a big impact on your life. They are the four adjustments you are about to read about in this section.

Without the ability to drop your intention and focus on connection, the other person just becomes a pawn in your chess game.

CHAPTER ONE

# Non-attachment

It was 20 years ago. After seven years at university, I eventually arrived in the real world. I was fortunate enough to land my first job with a fast-growing high-tech company. I had no experience writing software, but they reasoned that based on my mathematical aptitude, I could quickly learn. They were wrong. I quickly became a second-rate programmer. Fortunately for me, the company came to realize that I might be better with people than with lines of code.

Within 18 months I had a senior role, reporting to the general manager, Graham Orphan. Graham was a rare breed of general manager, both in appearance and capability. He had a blond Afro like Art Garfunkel's in the 1960s, a thin moustache and a habit of only ever wearing short-sleeved business shirts.

I remember walking into his office one day and, with all the blunt enthusiasm of youth, saying something like, "Graham, as a company we are doing some things wrong. But listen, I've got some ideas about how we can change things, so we can win more sales in North America."

He tolerated my bluntness and considered my ideas. But what he did next shocked me. He said, "I'm giving you 15 minutes at this Friday's senior management team meeting to share your ideas with the team."

I was excited. This was my big opportunity. And I set about preparing the best presentation possible.

Friday came. I walked in and surveyed the eighth-floor boardroom full of company founders, directors and other senior managers. They looked back at me with mildly encouraging smiles.

I fired up my presentation. And let me tell you how well I did.

At the start their smiles were mildly encouraging. By the end, their smiles were non-existent. I'd even turned the supportive ones against me.

I left the room dejected. But just before I left, Graham pulled me aside. He asked, "Daniel. Do you understand why that didn't go well for you?" I replied, "I guess they weren't ready to hear what I had to say."

He said, "That wasn't the problem. You cared too much about your point of view. And not enough about any of them. You need to care more for your audience than your outcome."

I said "That's good, Graham – care for the people not the outcome. I'll do that next time." He said, "I was hoping you'd say that. Next time is next Friday's senior management team meeting. I'll see you there." I thought to myself, "It's not often in business you're handed the chance to screw up twice in one week."

Next Friday arrived. I looked around the eighth-floor boardroom. Same company founders, directors and senior managers. Same frowns I'd etched onto their faces the week before. I took a deep breath – and ran out of the room. No, no. I did the presentation.

This time, everything was different. They began nodding their heads. And the reason that in October 1998, as a graduate just 18 months into working for the company, I found myself in charge of 36 people on my first multi-million-dollar project charged with overhauling the way the company delivered software was that simple, almost trite-sounding recommendation from Graham.

Graham understood that the core determinant of influence was that you must *care more about the other person than you do about your outcome.* He also understood that if you don't care, you must make yourself care, or nothing you say to them is going to matter.

On reading this story, you might be thinking, "That's a great reminder, but of course I would never screw up as badly as you did." You're probably right. You probably wouldn't get it as badly wrong as I did. However, there is a danger in this way of thinking. Of all the clients I've worked with, few have been truly unattached to their outcome. And a small attachment is like a small cancerous tumor – it is deadly, irrespective of size.

It's easy to see the theoretical value of being unattached, but to commit to consciously placing your attachment to one side and focusing on connecting to the person or people in that room – even when the conversation goes in a different direction to your hopes – requires effort.

Because to know but not to use, is not to know, I am going to ask that you connect to more than the theoretical value of non-attachment before you read any more of this book. Commit now to consciously adjusting your perspective in the direction of non-attachment before each pitch until this becomes an automatic habit. This one adjustment changes destiny.

John, a client of mine, was completing a multi-million-dollar investment raise. We'd done the pre-work to make his company investible, raised his ability to communicate value and made him tactically smart and more confident in the delivery of a message. But all this training would have gone to waste if we'd not also anticipated the need for non-attachment.

Because of how the investment unfolded, it was past the eleventh hour and he had still not received final signatures from his investor. Because of that, his business bank account ticked over into overdraft. Had the investor pulled out then, his company would have had no investment and no cash. He'd heard stories of hostile investors waiting until a company ran out of money and was desperate, then renegotiating terms. He'd heard stories of investors pulling out completely – just days before the money was due to be deposited in the bank.

John remained calm. He continued to expect the best and to know that no matter what happened, he'd find a way to continue. The investment arrived, and the investor-CEO relationship has been one of the best I've encountered.

Months later, John confided that of all he'd learned about pitching, the lesson on non-attachment had been the most important. He said that without that perspective, at best, that last week would have been intolerably stressful. At worst, he stood a serious risk of acting out of fear and attachment and causing the result he dreaded most.

If the notion of non-attachment sounds Eastern, that's because it is. One of the key reasons most Western approaches to sales, influence and pitching are incomplete and ineffective is that they are only just starting to grapple with something that has been understood in the East for millennia: Do not attach to the fruit of your actions.

Steve Jobs, the CEO of what became the largest company in the world by market capitalization, Apple, attributed much of his success to what he learned about influencing others, and himself, on an extended trip to India. When a young Mark Zuckerburg turned to Steve for advice when his company was going through tough times, Steve encouraged Mark to travel to India to spend time in an ashram. That trip proved pivotal to Mark's success. India was to play a vital role in my entrepreneurial journey too. In my case, though, India came to me. In early 2004, after months of trying, I'd finally turned a presentation to investors into a decision to enter due diligence.

I'd never even heard of due diligence before. It sounded serious and rigorous. It was. In terms of skillset, I was wholly unprepared for the specificity, directness and sharpness of the questions that a team of four investors would ask me during that meeting two weeks after our pitch. Fortunately, at the level of mindset, I'd undergone the perfect preparation.

As luck would have it, during that two-week gap between our successful pitch and the follow-up due diligence meeting, I was booked to spend two weeks organizing a tour and flying around the country with none other than Sri Sri Ravi Shankar (Sri Sri as he's affectionately known). Sri Sri is a multiple nominee for the Nobel Peace Prize, and according to *Forbes* magazine, is one of the most powerful influencers in India. He's what's known in the East as a fully realized master. I was excited at the opportunity. I'd never been up close to a living master before, let alone had the chance to travel with one, talk to one and observe one offstage.

What I learned during that time was the power of presence and the power of non-attachment to the fruits of your labors, and about how to set strong intentions that were likely to come to pass. But more than that, I simply learned more about how to be.

On one occasion, I was in the kitchen preparing breakfast at the homestead where Sri Sri and his travelling entourage, including me, were staying. I suddenly became aware that someone was cooking next to me. I turned to my left, and it was Sri Sri himself completely focused on frying up some zucchinis with spices. Another time he walked into the living area where a grand piano was stationed. He seated himself at the piano and began playing. And I mean playing, being playful with the piano – dancing his fingers like a mischievous cat – in a way that had us all laughing and wanting more.

What on earth does this experience have to do with pitching? Everything. By the time due diligence came, I felt happy for no reason. I wanted investment, but I trusted that whatever happened was for the best, and I simply wanted to do my best. I still remember vividly to this day being asked some of the bluntest questions I'd ever been asked about why I believed our company could succeed.

I remember knowing that as a rookie entrepreneur, I had no experience and no logical basis on which to give the investors an assurance that we would succeed. And yet, in that state of complete non-attachment, I seemed intuitively to know exactly what to say to every single investor present.

At the end – which only took 45 minutes – there was silence. I recall the look of surprise on the face of one of the investors as though he'd expected a knock-out in minutes. But the underdog was not only still standing, but ready to go another 12 rounds.

The lead investor paused, and said, "Well, it looks like you've given us no reason not to invest. Let's have a final meeting in another two weeks where we'll make our decision."

A few months later, I had one of my best post-investment pitch successes during my time at Helix8 when Aki von Roy agreed to join our board. Aki was the former European Union president of Bristol Myers Squibb. He'd run the entire European arm of one the world's largest pharmaceutical companies. He managed 7000 people and a multi-billion-dollar budget. During one of our lunchtime catch-ups I was talking about non-attachment with him. He listened with eyes closed, head down and furrowed brow – his trademark pose of utter concentration. When I finished, he remained silent for some time. At last he spoke, recounting the following anecdote.

"Let me tell you what happened when I started off in the pharmaceutical industry. We were all given sales rep training.

At my first post-training meeting, I was supposed to physically position products close to the doctors I was selling to. If they moved them, we were instructed to move the product back near them again. I asked the top salespeople at the company whether the sales training worked. They all said it didn't and told me to just be myself.

"The second meeting I went in and just made a connection, started talking about the weather and said, 'This is just the second time I've done this, so I might stuff up, but let's just have a chat.' At the end, I said, 'By the way, they want me to leave this with you.' 'What's that?' asked the doctor. 'It's a suppository – it's supposed to be quite good,' I said. 'Leave it with me,' replied the doctor."

That was Aki's way of saying, "I agree with you. Most people are taught to be attached, but actually the opposite works better." I was grateful he'd shared it in a story – not a statement.

## Care for others not the outcome

Becoming unattached happens *before* you step into that room. First, you must know with certainty that your attachment to an outcome makes that outcome less likely to occur, not more.

Second, you must decide that you have done all the work you can, and that from now on your task is to remain present and care for the other person.

I had an incantation I used repeatedly until it became automatic for me to care more about the other person than my outcome. It went as follows.

"I now invoke through my will everything I need in my body, mind and spirit to serve this person to my maximum potential, to get any remaining doubt or ego out of the way and to leave it all on the field to inspire them to transformative results from the heart."

You may simplify the incantation to "I am committed to the other person above and beyond my outcome" or if you are more visual, you can use the following sequence:

1. Visualize a picture that represents your intended outcome.

2. Allow that image to dissolve.

3. Replace it with an image of you communicating with care to your audience, without attachment.

Non-attachment does not mean being aloof. The clients who are the most successful at winning pitches, who win more than 80 percent of pitches they make, share what I call mental swagger. Mental swagger is the attitude of, "We like you and we'd love to help you. But if you don't want the same thing, it's no big deal."

## Questions

- Can you remember the last sales situation where the salesperson obviously cared more about their agenda than you? Was their pitch successful?

- Have you ever failed to influence because you cared too much for your cause?

- When was the last time you sought to influence someone without first considering how they might listen to you?

- Do you think that if your mindset is not to drop your *in*tention and focus on *con*nection, the other person notices that they are pawn in your chess game?

Intention is the necessary first step that guarantees the focus and the boldness of your message will be strong enough to ignite the inspired actions of others.

# CHAPTER 2

# Intention

By my third round of capital raising as CEO of Helix8, my goal was no longer simply to raise capital. I decided my intention for that pitch was to raise capital within six weeks from investors who were truly inspired to invest in us.

Because of the presence of the word *inspired* in my intention, it led to a different sort of pitch. It forced me to take bolder actions, speak with greater enthusiasm, make more powerful choices at key moments, be a better storyteller, be more succinct and communicate in a way that was not only influential, but visionary.

At the end of the pitch I glanced over the feedback that had been given by prospective investors. The most commonly occurring piece of feedback was the word *inspiring*. It was as though my intention had flowed through me into my words and then into the minds of my audience, and from there into the feedback they put on the page – and yes, into their decision to invest. Because of my strong intention, we got investors who not only had money, but who shared our vision and were excited to do whatever they could to help us win.

When writing this book, I also set intentions. My key intention was to have 100,000 people or more *read and implement* the principles in this book *to change the world for the better*. The boldness of this intention forced me to write in a bolder way, making stronger demands of my readers.

The boldness of this intention required me to speak more directly, to be more compassionate, to use more inspiring stories than ever before. It has demanded that I embody the principles of this book in my writing at every juncture.

The intention about gaining not just readers, but implementers, has required me to include non-standard aspects in this book. It has required me to include questions at the end of each chapter designed to help you overcome any limiting beliefs that could stop you from implementing what you have just read.

It has required me to ask you to reflect on your responsibility as a good person to make sure you gain great influence and to share these ideas generously. It has required me to do everything I can to help you achieve your dreams, aspirations and goals *during* your lifetime, so you don't end up regretting the gap between your dreams and reality at the *end* of your lifetime.

This intention required me to make bold claims and then provide evidence for each of them. So, while your intention starts within you, it flows through into your behaviors in the form of your mindset, message, tactics and delivery. These behaviors then flow through into the consequences for those who experience them.

## Ignite inspiration

When should you set an intention? Intention is the first act of creating a pitch. It precedes designing a message, it precedes writing your presentation and it even precedes thinking about who your audience is and what they might need to hear to be influenced by you.

So, what sort of intention should you have?

First, your intention should be primarily about serving others. In fact, having a service-based intention is your guarantee of not becoming overly anxious or nervous during your pitch.

Thought leader Matt Church calls this "going from nervous to service." Feeling nervous is a sign that your focus is in the wrong place. It's on you and your performance. You are concerned about whether your performance will meet up to your expectations. But to your audience, that is irrelevant. They don't know what your script is, how you've prepared and whether what you say measures up to your internal expectations. All they care about is whether you show up powerfully and that they feel more energized at the end of your pitch than they did at the beginning.

Your choice is between lying on your deathbed, feeling regret and wondering 'what if?' or living an amazing life in which you have manifested your dreams.

Feeling nervous and anxious about your performance is in fact a great way to guarantee they'll experience the opposite of this, that they will be more likely to feel enervated by your self-obsession.

So how should you form an intention? Simple. Remove all other distractions and ask yourself, "What is the most powerful intention that I could have for the outcome of this pitch?" By practicing this powerful question repeatedly, you are always guided immediately to the strongest intention, not just for you, but for the other person and therefore the world.

A service-based intention could sound like the following. "I aim to provide a great opportunity for the right customers to see how our product could powerfully serve them and their business, so that they feel inspired to take immediate action that will benefit them the most in the shortest time frame possible."

When I am taking on new coaching clients, I have a strategy session of up to one hour with prospects. My intention for the strategy session, which is partly a qualification process and partly a pitch, is to find out whether this person could become a great client with whom I could create a partnership based on a conspiracy to succeed. I'm looking for a partnership so strong that by the end of the call, it's obvious to both of us that we should work together, and I'm not wondering whether we will achieve results, I'm excited about the results that I'm confident we will achieve together.

Similarly, my intention is to quickly diagnose whether the person is not a good fit, so I can let them know that before entering a coaching relationship. Because of the power of this intention, it has been more than a year since I've taken on board any uncommitted clients, and every client who has come on board has indeed achieved powerful results in a ridiculously short amount of time.

Another of my intentions is that I not only find great clients, but also that I bring out the best in them, including activating their highest standards from the first conversation. My philosophy is that through your intention to bring out the best in someone, you succeed at bringing out the best in them. It works in the same way that a child at school may behave in five different ways for five different teachers, based on how much each teacher has the intention to bring out the highest standard in that child.

When your intention is only to tolerate the best standards from someone and to hold them to account to their highest potential, people will either disqualify themselves or meet that bar willingly. Either way, the result is speed and excellence.

It is this intention to work only with committed people and to show them the standard required from the first conversation that has been half the reason for the unbroken chain of incredibly successful client results I've had over the past two years.

## Questions

- What is the cost of not setting your intention before you begin any pitch, and how does this lead to a watered-down version of your power and impact?

- How committed are you to doing this consistently before every single pitch?

- If two minutes spent sending a powerful intention requires you to take bolder actions to show up more for others, to be a fuller version of yourself and consequently achieve greater results, why would you not take this time consistently?

- Can you see examples in your life of where your pitches were weak because you did not set a strong intention?

- Can you see how in the past you became nervous because you didn't set a service-based intention?

- What could your intention be for your next pitch in terms of how it serves other people and your own vision?

# CHAPTER 3

# Growth Mindset

Imagine how excited I was in 2003 when the New Zealand Trade Development Board arranged for me to pitch at the University of California's San Diego Connect program, one of the world's most successful stages for marrying entrepreneurs with capital. If you had been with me in San Diego on 3 September that year, you would have seen a life-changing sequence of events. I was suited and booted and I looked sharp. I opened the door and I saw everyone else was in Hawaiian shirts and board shorts.

My clothes were saying, "I've dressed to impress." Their clothes were saying, "I no longer have to impress anyone."

Inside those shirts and shorts were individuals who between them had witnessed more than a thousand investment pitches. The room contained probably well over US$1 billion of net worth from people who had led multiple successful companies, and who had the means to propel an entrepreneur's company to the next level, if the pitch was good enough.

I'd read about the importance of visualizing the outcome you want. So, I had visualized these people saying "that was great" at the end of my pitch and deciding then and there to open their checkbooks.

To complete this visualization process, once I entered the room, I zoned in on the hardest-to-impress looking investor I could find, a poker-faced, bespectacled and bearded man named Jay Kunin. He looked like a hard-nosed version of the movie director Peter Jackson. In my mind's eye, I visualized him fixing his eye on me at the end of my pitch. In my mind's ear, I heard him say, "That was great" and committing to invest.

This is what happened next. I had just finished my pitch. There was pin-drop silence. My heart was pounding. I was roasting inside my jacket. Then Jay, exactly as I visualized, squinted at me, peered over his glasses and said three fateful words. "Was that it?"

That wasn't the phrase I'd written for him in my visualization. He continued. "If your technology is as good as you say it is, what's to stop a better-funded team here in California overtaking you in six months?"

I knew how to handle this. I looked him in the eye, and I said "Jay. That's a good question. I don't have an answer for you right now. But I'd be happy to get back to you in a couple of days with the answer you seek." It's the sort of evasive answer you give when you're stumped and are trying to minimize damage.

Then the woman, a venture capitalist, sitting next to him, began. "Given that academics are notoriously hard to sell to, how do you know that your cost of sale won't be more than your buy price?" I can't even remember what I said. But it wasn't good.

What followed was a 20-minute tag-team mauling by 12 dragons in Hawaiian shirts, where I learned that my product was one of the most problematic they had seen. I was a lot further from realizing my idea than I'd hoped.

They were friendly enough when I left, and even invited me back once I had more answers (something they did to everyone, no matter how bad their pitch was). I felt so crushed that by the time I'd stumbled back onto the plane, I'd already begun rationalizing to myself reasons to give up. Of course, I didn't admit that to myself at the time. But that's exactly what I had started doing.

Bad as that was, it was what happened next back in New Zealand that shocked me. I told Roger, my business coach, what had happened. He looked at me through his brown beady eyes and asked, "So, what's next?"

I opened my mouth and started telling the lies that anyone starts telling themselves when they are starting to give up on their dream, lies that sound innocent, realistic and logical – but are in fact toxic to our growth and suffocating to our dreams.

"Well it's just too hard to get investment. And without investment, I can't fully commit right now. But it'll still be on the slow burner." What he said next changed the direction of my life.

He said, "Dan, in their feedback they gave you a *recipe for success*. You're seeing it as an indictment of failure. You left your job for this idea. Ever since I've known you this is all you've talked about. This idea is your baby. If you stop feeding it, it'll die. Your idea does not deserve to die!"

Most people think the number one thing that gets between them and their idea reaching its potential is an obstacle on the outside – the economy, lack of resources, lack of capital, lack of proximity to market. That's not it. That's the lies we tell ourselves. *What stops our idea reaching its potential is when we decide to stop feeding it.* Because when that baby called your idea needs feeding, sometimes even tomorrow is too late.

I said, "See that's why you're my coach – my idea does not deserve to die. I'm going back into the dragon's den." And I found another group to pitch to. And they also tore apart my pitch. But this time they didn't find nearly as much at fault. This time, I heard their feedback as a recipe for change, not an indictment of failure.

I kept on pitching, until nine months later I was invited into a room of angel investors who had just completed one month of due diligence on our company after hearing my pitch. The lead investor opened his mouth and said, "We're in."

That group was called ICE Angels. As it turned out, they were making their first ever investment. Today they are New Zealand's largest seed investment group. And today, the company they funded is one of New Zealand's more successful high-tech companies. It has changed the way that molecular biologists do research around the world.

I have not lost an investment pitch or tender since then, and at the time of writing, my average client pitch win rate is more than 85 percent. So, the advice my coach gave me was very special – your idea does not deserve to die.

## Use feedback to fuel success

Pitches are pivots because they are moments in time where your destiny follows a different path – a higher and grander path – because you have risen to the occasion. With the help of my coach,

Seeing feedback as a recipe for success is what creates a growth mindset.

I rose to a higher purpose than the one I would have followed had I not listened to his tough-to-hear words.

In that moment, I pivoted from being a man with a *fixed* mindset to being a man with a *growth* mindset.

Rather than sharing this story, I could have cited the brilliant research that the Carol Dweck has done on growth mindset and published in her book *Mindset: The New Psychology of Success*. But it would not have been as valuable to you. That's her story, not mine. I believe that all you need to understand right here and right now in the context of pitching until you change the world is that *you have a choice.*

If you get feedback that is negative, you could choose to believe it means either:

- the people giving the feedback should be discounted, or

- the people giving the feedback have provided evidence that you don't have it in you to do what you wanted.

Either way, you will not want to do more of the thing that got you that less-than-positive feedback. You'll either give up or blame others – without improving what you do. Giving up is what I was about to do, and is what instantly kills many dreams. Blaming others keeps your dream on life support – where they will stay until you start taking responsibility.

The third choice is to do what my coach suggested I do – see feedback as a recipe for success, not an indictment of failure. This is what creates a growth mindset.

Once you decide to have a growth mindset, everything becomes a game. Even in the face of negative feedback, you think, "Great – I know what to do next time." You know with certainty that through the simple process of hearing feedback and iterating or continuing to repeat your pitch, it is almost inevitable that you will achieve the result you seek.

In the Mastermind group I run for technology CEOs, I use this principle relentlessly. Growth mindset, decisiveness and some core abilities are the three criteria that must be present for me to begin coaching someone. Without a growth mindset, the chances of transformative results are low. With a growth mindset, almost anything can be achieved.

Why? Because the ability to see failure as feedback means that no matter what other skills are missing in a person, over time they will be filled in because that person is open to hearing feedback and using it to improve over and over again, until success is gained.

Imagine what would happen if children did not have a growth mindset. Would a baby ever learn to walk? All people start off with a growth mindset. We cannot grow and develop without one. So, *growth-mindset is already inside you* – it's simply a matter of you deciding to access it and behave differently in the face of apparent setbacks until you re-establish this natural pattern of interacting with the world.

## Questions

- What idea have you stopped feeding?

- What sort of parent are you to your idea? A committed one or an impatient foster parent, ready to give your baby back if it doesn't meet your expectations right away?

- What innocent-sounding logic do you sell yourself when you are in fact playing small because you've had a setback?

# CHAPTER 4

# Conviction

Before you can change the world for the better, you must first *believe* that you can change the world.

This belief cannot be faked – you must really believe that you can change the world. So how do you do that if you don't currently feel that way? The answer is ridiculously easy.

The key is in the subtlety of language. You must believe that you *can* change the world, not believe that you *will*. The belief that you can, leads to the belief that you will. Possibility precedes inevitably. Always.

The simplest way to know with certainty that you can change the world for the better is to accept that the opposite of this belief is nonsense. Can you stare in the face of the opposite belief that it is impossible for you to change the world for the better and see that as a ridiculous thing to believe? In other words, believe that it is impossible that *it is impossible* for you to change the world.

No matter how much self-doubt, or lack of skill, resources or prior track record of success you have, knowing this fact renders you no different from any other person near the start of their journey who went on to change the world for the better. None of these other things matter as much as your belief that this is possible.

This, along with every element of pitching in this book, was something I had to learn experientially. At the age of 12 I was terrified of, and very bad at, speaking in front of a group. I realized that before I could speak in front of a group, I must *believe it was possible* for me to do so. I focused on believing this, and within 12 months I heard with disbelief when in front of 560 kids the principal announced, "And the winner of the [Year 7] speech competition is ... Daniel Batten."

So, what does matter? What matters is your conviction that it is possible for you to change the world for the better.

Perhaps you're in a company and you cannot see how your role in it is going to lead to positive change in the world. All this means is that you haven't yet stretched your imagination enough. So long as your product or service is providing something that is not negative to the world, your legacy will not be your product or service, but the impact you have in your interactions with the people whose lives you touch. These people will be your customers, your team and other people you meet through your travels.

It is my conviction and my experience that anyone who believes they can change the world for the better, can.

In my conviction and my experience, the fastest way to grow a company is to grow the person running it. And it is also my conviction and my experience that the fastest way to grow a person is to grow their ability to pitch. Because, by growing your ability to pitch, you can change the trajectory of many key pivot points in your life.

I am now certain that this is true and that through my actions I have already helped to change the world for the better. Conviction knows no limits, so I will continue to do this at even greater magnitude.

However, there was a time when I was not certain. There was a time when this was only a seed of possibility. Then, it was enough that I believed it was possible that through the work I do, I could change the world for the better. This seed of possibility meant that results were possible. As the results came in, they reinforced the belief, turning possibility into probability and probability into certainty.

When it came to pitching, there was a time when I used to rely on the strength of my case to convince people. Convincing is the opposite of conviction. Convincing implies you are trying to use logic to get people to think as you think.

Conviction means you have a wholehearted belief that the side of truth is with you and that your task is one of compassion to help someone see this truth. With a mindset of conviction, immature desires, such as the desire to entertain, to be one of the club, to be liked or to be perceived a certain way, fall away.

American television personality Fred Rogers delivered one of the greatest pitches of all time on 1 May 1969. In less than seven minutes he convinced a skeptical senator to unleash US$20 million of funding for the US public broadcasting service. He had no well-argued case, no documented evidence, statistics or data. So, what did he have? Just a simple story, a poem and most importantly, utter conviction in his cause.

Your first exercise in this chapter is to watch this pitch. Search YouTube for Fred Rogers testifying before the Senate Subcommittee on Communications.

Conviction cannot be faked. It must be felt. Conviction is closely linked to what thought-leader Simon Sinek, in his book *Start with Why: How Great Leaders Inspire Everyone to Take Action*, calls "your why". It is the reason that people who follow their passion are more likely to be successful than those who do not. Because without conviction, which is the twin sister of following your passion, your chance of influencing others is drastically reduced.

The bold claims at the beginning of this book are an expression of conviction. Without my conviction that *the* most under-used way to change the direction of your destiny is to learn how to pitch, this book and its focus on what to do differently would have been impossible.

When working with entrepreneurs, I start by asking people why they are doing what they are doing. The answer to this question is often surprising and bigger than you might expect.

I asked myself this question when writing this book. My answer was that there is an even bigger purpose than helping adults to change the world for the better through the strength of their pitch.

It is my conviction that until we revolutionize key and core parts of our education system, we will continue to educate children for a world that does not exist, leaving them badly unprepared for the world that does. Not only that, I believe that until we revolutionize our education system, 90 percent of adults will continue to believe they can only be happy once they achieve some distant goal, yet at the same time doubt their capacity to achieve that goal.

I am not talking about *de*-schooling society. I am talking about *re*-schooling society. These schools of the near future will have oratory and rhetoric back in, they will have mindset training in and they will have personal and leadership development in.

I believe this goal is possible. And I believe what makes this future possible is the fact that it is not ideology but necessity that will drive the urgent need for these changes.

## Create commitment

So, what can you do to experience greater conviction in the next pitch you give?

1.  After you have watched the Fred Rogers' clip, ask yourself "*Why* am I doing what I am doing? What is the greater reason?" Changing the world could simply mean changing your part of the world, experiencing greater connection or freedom with your family, greater time freedom or having a more positive impact on other people wherever you go.

    I've expressed my answer to this question in the form of pledges. I have one pledge relating to my work in the world and another pledge to my family.

# MY PLEDGE TO MY WORK IN THE WORLD

*"I will be 100 percent myself come what may, for myself, my family and the world.*

*I commit to usher forth Leader 2.0:*

- *in as many Kiwi innovators as it takes for us to reasonably lift our gross domestic confidence*

- *in as many business leaders as it takes to make happy workers the norm*

- *in as many children as it takes to make their burning question be not, 'What job should I do?', but 'What gifts do I share?'*

*I commit to this path:*

- *even though it may be long*

- *even though others may doubt its size*

- *even though I may not always know the path ahead.*

*I commit to this vision:*

- *even if I have setbacks*

- *even if it is uncomfortable*

- *even if I do not yet have all the resources to create it.*

*I will not rest until either this vision comes to pass or death takes me.*

*I will do whatever it takes to realize this vision, fulfil my purpose and honor my legacy.*

*Signed: Daniel Batten"*

# MY PLEDGE TO MY FAMILY

*"I commit to bringing leadership to my family:*
- *to be great as a husband and father*
- *to hold myself to a higher standard than my family holds me.*

*I will bring to my family:*
- *quality time, care and shared experiences that are fun and transformational*
- *planning ways to grow as a unit and as individuals*
- *all of me.*

*I am committed to my family experiencing the most energetic version of me.*

*I am committed to the supporting habits and routines that will deliver that energy.*

*Each month, there will be:*
- *a time to meet and decide what we want to experience as a family, and*
- *a special event [as] Dad with each of my children.*

*To my kids, I shall ask not, 'What can I role model based on what I've experienced?', but 'What can I role model that I may never have experienced?'*

*To my wife, I shall ask not, 'How can I give her what she wants?', but 'How can I give her what it may never have occurred to her to ask for?'*

*I am committed to this path because I want my family to receive and I want to be the best husband and father possible.*

*Signed: Daniel Batten"*

2. When you give your next pitch, get clear on not only the immediate decision you want the other person to make, but the *reason* you want them to make that decision – the higher reason. For me it is not enough that a person decides in the direction that serves them and me, I also want them to make that decision *from the most committed part of their being.* This is impossible unless I bring to the conversation *the most committed part of my being.*

Two years ago, I attended a gathering of business owners in the software sector in New Zealand. The five of us there for the first time at that club's monthly meeting were invited to get up and each say a few words about what we were doing. The others got up and talked about what they did. There were plenty of acronyms and jargon along the way. After they had finished, the person sitting next to me said, "Half of them I couldn't understand. The other half I couldn't understand why anyone would care."

Then I got up and said, "My name's Daniel and I believe that in our country there is more value to be milked from the minds of the smart people like you in this room than there is to be milked from the udders of our cows."

Being in New Zealand, where the largest export earner was dairy, not technology, there were several "hear, hear" responses. I continued. "I'm committed to working with smart Kiwi entrepreneurs to help to unleash this value so that New Zealand can have technology as its major export earner in the next 10 years."

From those 20 seconds of conviction, three people came up afterwards and asked what I did – three prospective clients. One of those prospective clients was Ollie, who you read about in Section 1: Mindset and will hear more about in Chapter 16: Story.

Without those 20 seconds of conviction I would not have met Ollie. He would not have turned around his pitch. And he would not have changed the transport direction of a nation.

When I started coaching other high-tech entrepreneurs, I released a hand-held video recorded on an iPhone4 of me in the backyard, with wind distorting the sound and the light settings changing constantly. Content-wise, the video had almost no script

– just three points, one story and one key metaphor. But it did have one ton of conviction. I put the video on Facebook, and that one piece of raw conviction resulted in not only two of the first clients for my newly formed Mastermind group, but a whole lot of supporters for the cause I had let the world know I cared about.

Conviction is such a powerful force that it can forgive other weaknesses. I'm not suggesting that you be lazy and rely on conviction to stop polishing where the format demands polish. But sometimes raw is what is demanded of the occasion. In these cases, conviction is what will make the rawness work powerfully.

# Questions

- Have you pretended to yourself that this chapter is not for you? Maybe you're thinking, "I'm just working for a company that sells $x$ – no great cause there," or, the opposite, "Yes, I already know that."

- Are those beliefs examples of a growth mindset or a fixed mindset?

- What more useful thing could you decide to believe instead?

If you are trying to sabotage your application of this chapter, ask yourself:

- "How could I have conviction in what I do?"

- "How does what I/we do change people's lives for the better?"

- "What stories of success do I need to get better at sharing so I can see and increase how I help people?"

TACTICS

One postgraduate degree in English, one diploma in drama and zero training in technology is not the usual path for a technology entrepreneur.

On one hand, my training in English and drama gave me an advantage when pitching, because I knew some vital things that others in business didn't know about message and delivery. But on the other hand, it led me to a dangerous conclusion.

For many years, I falsely assumed that message and delivery were the only two parts of pitching that were important. If I was surprised years later to discover how important mindset was, I was truly alarmed to find out that sometimes the right tactical maneuvers could be more powerful than what I'd spent years learning as an actor or linguist.

The first person who taught me this was Harvey. I was left admiring this young man who achieved in seven minutes something that negated his three years of university underachievement.

Harvey was one of 34 prospective software developers who had applied for a job at Helix 8. At the time, he was, literally, flipping burgers at McDonalds. Unlike the other 33 people who had submitted their CVs to us, Harvey did something different. He somehow found my number and rang me. The conversation went like this.

Harvey: "Hi, Daniel, this is Harvey here."

Me: "Who?"

Harvey: "Harvey. I supplied my CV to you in response to the software developer position you have advertised."

Me: "Oh, yeah, um, OK. Hang on, Harvey. I have the pile here. Let me just quickly check."

At that time, I had no idea how to filter through job applicants and so my co-founder and I had decided that to get the numbers down, the first filter would be based on university grades. We'd selected three piles. Pile A, students who had 'A's; Pile B, students who had 'B's; Pile C, everyone else.

I started looking through the A pile, assuming that he must be there, judging by the conviction in his voice that he should have heard back from me by now. I didn't find his CV in Pile A. I didn't find his CV in Pile B. I found his CV halfway through Pile C.

Harvey, as it turned out, had been pretty much a C student. He'd got the odd B- and failed a few papers.

Me: "Well, Harvey, your grades were not that great. We weren't even considering looking at you." Harvey had anticipated this response.

Harvey: "I know what you're saying and you're right. My grades weren't good. However, I believe passionately that my ideal environment is the workplace, not a lecture theatre. Something about university was not the condition in which I could thrive; it felt artificial. If you just give me a chance to prove myself I know I can do exceptional software development for you."

Me: "Well, Harvey, that's a good pitch. You may be right, but it's a costly mistake to us if you're wrong, so, we're not going to interview you. But I'll tell you what I am prepared to do. Because I admire you for having the guts to ring me up, we're going to give you a small programming task to do in your own time. I'm not making any guarantees, but if what you supply us with is at the standard you claim you're capable of, we'll consider you for an interview."

He profusely thanked me. We gave him the task. He did well. We gave him an aptitude test. Again, he did well – very well. We decided to interview him. We liked him. He had the attitude we wanted. He was outside the box. We also got to see that the reasons he would not have thrived in an academic environment were the very reasons he would thrive in ours. But there was one final hurdle – he still had to get past Mark.

Mark was our top programmer. Because of what I still regard as our most important pitch win at Helix8, on a third try we had eventually succeeded in getting an award-winning programmer –

and the top programmer in the country in our view – to join our team. Due to too much gaming in the 1990s, Mark had Occupational Overuse Syndrome in his hands and so programmed using voice recognition software. We endearingly referred to him as the Stephen Hawking of Helix8. He remains the best programmer I've ever met, and he is one of the big reasons that we were successful.

It was Harvey's final trial. He sat nervously next to Mark, slightly in awe of him, while Mark gave him a real programming task to do in less than an hour. I sat just a couple of desks away. It was a tense hour for everyone.

At the end of the task, Harvey left. I looked at Mark. Mark nodded his head, and said laconically, "Yep – he's pretty good." A few minutes later, I called Harvey and said, "You're in."

More than 10 years later, Harvey is still at the company. He's a team leader and one of the key members of the Helix8 team who have taken our product global. Compare that to where he was at the time – McDonalds. How different his path would have been without the bold move of picking up the phone and giving me the answer he did to my reason for not getting back to him.

Tactics had won Harvey a new destiny. And how long had he spent on the phone with me that day? Less than seven minutes. Over the next 10 years, I encountered several instances where a conversation of around seven minutes changed the destiny of a person or a company.

There are a lot of tactical adjustments that matter very little to the number of pitches you win. But there are four tactical adjustments that will make a big impact on the number of pitches you win and therefore a big impact on your life. They are the four adjustments you are about to read about in this section.

# CHAPTER 5

# Anticipation

Your pitch is a conversation, not a presentation. Even if you're talking to a large crowd, it's still a conversation, not a presentation.

Most people are fooled into believing that their pitch is not a conversation simply because they cannot hear the other person's responses. In a presentation, you better believe that the person is having responses to everything you are saying. You just can't *hear* these responses. But you can *anticipate* them.

Your audience will always ask you questions in their head, and you can control the types of questions they ask. In fact, you have almost complete control.

For example, you can anticipate a lot of the objections they will have and not only what objections they will have, but when they will have them. By anticipating what naysayers will say and then directly tackling these objections, you can very quickly take away the power of any unspoken objections and provide the skeptic with the feeling that you can read their mind. This is a powerful empathy-building tool. It is also a powerful leadership tool.

Anticipating how your audience will think takes conscious effort. That conscious effort is an expression of the fact that you've cared enough about them to imagine how they might respond to you. In other words, anticipation shows you care.

If ever there was a practical way to respond to the adage 'people don't care how much you know until they know how much you care', it is through the rule of anticipation. Only a couple of days ago, I was coaching a client on how to successfully win his pitch through using the rule of anticipation.

This client, Shaun, is an academic who wanted to set up his

own company to commercialize some of the incredible discoveries his research team had made. His department was underfunded and every person in that department had a high teaching load. For his departmental head, the thought of losing one of their most competent teachers was not a pleasant one. I worked with Shaun on the principle of anticipation so that we could pre-empt this objection before it was even raised. What he said was along the following lines.

"I'm convinced that the best way to move this forward is for us to set up a spinoff company and commercialize the IP we have created. I realize that this has certain consequences. For example, you may be thinking, 'but I'm going to lose a teacher if we do this.' It's my belief that far from the department losing a teacher, we will gain much, much more.

"Firstly, we will gain the kudos of taking intellectual property to the world. This will help us to earn a reputation with future students as a department that leverages the value of what gets created in the real world.

"Secondly, we will earn money directly through the value of the company we create, and as we know, when such a company exists, a sizeable portion of its value goes back to the department that established it. This money can be used to create many more teaching and research positions than we could possibly imagine.

"Thirdly, I see this as paving the way for professors of the present and the future to continue to leave a trail of excellence that continues to give back to this department and make it one of the highest performing departments in this university and perhaps in the country. This will reflect well on our brand and well on this department. It will enable us to do the research we love and more of the teaching we love, and it'll make everyone here, both today and in the future, into winners."

Because of Shaun's use of anticipation, his head of department could see his temporary small loss in the context of a potentially enormous future gain. Shaun not only neutralized his head of department's key concern, he gained an advocate within the university for forming his spinoff company.

## Anticipate objections

There are three steps to anticipating responses before they occur.

1. Test your message out on other people. Invite them to look at your idea from the point of view of a skeptic, that is, to imagine what could go wrong and to write down every objection they can think of.

2. Ask them to share these objections with you. Write down every single one.

3. In a separate column, write your answer to every single objection.

4. Imbed these answers into your pitch. If it's a significant objection, take some time to speak to it; if it's an important yet less pivotal objection, you may be able to handle it in a single sentence.

For example, if there is an objection about lack of experience in the team, you might say, "We have the passion and we have the product knowledge. The only thing we are lacking is experience. However, history tells us that the most successful entrepreneurs ever to walk this planet also started off their most successful companies in exactly the same position as us, with the same experience as us. I believe we are strongly positioned to take on the world and win."

Useful phrases to attend to anticipated objections include:

- You may be thinking ...

- You'd be forgiven for thinking ...

- We asked ourselves how we could do $x$ (where $x$ is an objection to something that sounds implausible).

# Questions

- Who can you test your message on?

- If you were to in the shoes of the person about to receive your pitch, what objections would you have?

- What are your own fears, hesitations and reservations?

- Where could you incorporate into your pitch the phrases suggested above to give people the impression you've read their mind?

In a pitch, the points for you are the moments of inspiration you create; the points against you are the risks you fail to counter.

# CHAPTER 6

# De-risking

When it comes to the psychology of decision making, it's useful to know that people decide emotionally but defend their decision logically. Risk triggers feelings of fear. And fear is like a cloud obscuring the sunlight of the win you are seeking. So, to bask in that sunlight, you must first remove the cloud of risk.

One of the major reasons good pitches fail to win hearts and minds is when they don't come across as low risk. In any game of sport, to win you must not only score points, you must stop the opponent from scoring points.

An inspiring pitch that fails to tackle risk is like an attacking sports team with a weak defense. It won't win. Many factors cause risk, but perhaps the biggest is the failure to have integrity. Integrity simply means that what you say equals what you do.

Everyone claims to have integrity, but few people demonstrate it – meaning very few do have it. To have integrity:

- you say something.
- you do something.
- what you say and what you do are the same.

The surprising result is that a lack of integrity can be caused not only by a failure to do something you said you would, but a *failure to tell someone what you did*.

Let me give you an example. Most people start their conversations too late. When they present an idea to another person, they are asking that person to make a decision the first time they meet. This is a weak tactic, which lacks integrity, because the other person has had no opportunity to see whether you are a person whose speech and actions are consistent.

## Start conversations early

So how is this solved? By starting conversations early. Rather than approach a person when everything is ready and ask them to make a decision then, talk to the person and start building a relationship beforehand.

If you have a product and you want to have a conversation with a customer or an investor, simply start the conversation before the product is ready. If you are pitching to an investor, this means saying the following.

"We don't have anything to show you just yet, but we will in three months' time. My purpose in reaching out to you today is two-fold. First, to let you know that we will have something in three months that we want to pitch to you. Second, when we do pitch this to you, we want to make sure our pitch is relevant. So, we'd like to let you know where we're at today, and to get your view on what gaps we need to close before we return. Is that fair enough?"

Now the nuances of what you say may change, but the spirit behind it will not. I've used this tactic to excite and create curiosity about a product or a share offering before later approaching the customer or investor again. The result was two-fold.

Firstly, the customer or investor was excited and pleasantly surprised that I had the honesty to admit we weren't ready to show them anything yet, and respected me not wasting their time pretending we did. Secondly, they really appreciated having the chance to be involved and have input before we approached them with the product or share offering.

Because of that, when we were ready, three other things happened.

1. Because we approached them in the time frame we said we would, we showed that what we said we would do and what we did were in alignment. In other words, we proved we had integrity.

2. Because it wasn't the first time we had met them, the relationship was already warm by the time we pitched.

3. Because we had been able to attend to points they had asked us to address, the pitch was not just our story, it was their story.

A second example of how to de-risk a pitch is something I became aware of over three weeks when I coached 25 teams of scientists in pitching. The common fault of every team was that they didn't make two points critical to an audience's decision making. They didn't say either:

1. This is what we've already done (that is, what we've already de-risked).

2. This is what we're going to try to do next (and how we'll use investment funding to get there).

The solution to this is the "this is what we've done ... this is what we're going to do" language structure. It goes like this.

1. Say, "These are the three critical commercial milestones we have achieved to date." Then name them.

2. Say, "These are the next three milestones we are going to achieve using the capital we gain." Then name them.

3. Say honestly how much risk is associated with each future milestone and how much you will have de-risked the company when you hit each one.

Now that may not strike you as the most inspiring way to present, but when it comes to risk, remember that de-risking a pitch is like the defending wall in a team sport – it won't inspire the masses, but you'll lose if you don't do it well.

It's not complex, flashy, super-maneuvers that are called for. De-risking is about stating the simple and direct facts that would otherwise cause your pitch to leak defensively through failing to mitigate perceived risk.

Just as a sports team relies on strong structures and patterns for defense, strong structures and patterns in your language are required to mount a strong defense for why your business is relatively low risk. This can also be represented in a slide and here is an image of how you might do that.

## Milestones over time

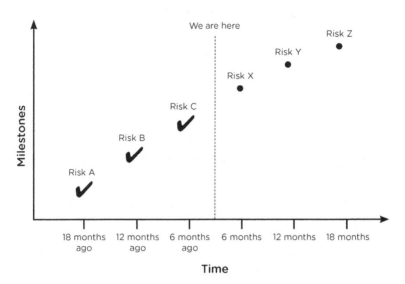

Time

Why this works so effectively is that it mentions what you've done and what you're about to do *together*.

In terms of the psychology of decision-making, the decision maker unconsciously processes the information they see and hear as follows.

"This person has already achieved three significant milestones. There are three more significant milestones to achieve. I can see all these milestones on their slide and in my mind. The most logical conclusion is that this person will continue to hit their milestones one by one."

This only works if you use the precise language structure I've outlined above. Remember, mention what you are going to achieve with that level of confidence immediately after you mention what you've already achieved. It's important that you state the risk factors and acknowledge that there is no certainty you will achieve your future milestones. Why? Because decision makers understand that the future is, by definition, uncertain. When *you* acknowledge the uncertainty, two critical things occur in the mind of the decision-maker.

1. Their level of trust in you goes up.

2. They will tend to believe your assessment about the relative level of risk involved.

## Questions

- What are the key risks in your pitch?

- What language structures can you create that would de-risk them?

- How have you unwittingly conveyed risk through what you failed to say, such as risks you didn't acknowledge or quantify, or milestones you have achieved?

- Where do you fail to be transparent?

- What is the likely consequence of your lack of transparency about risk? What will the impact be if the other party must dig to get answers? How will they feel if they later find a risk you didn't front up with?

# CHAPTER 7

# Momentum

When I was at Helix8, the time between our first pitch to the angel investment group and having investment in our bank was less than three months. In doing so, we ended up leap-frogging another company that had been in due diligence with the same investment group for about nine months.

The other company eventually got investment too, and I ended up on good terms with the CEO. Years later we compared our approaches to getting investment. It became clear that we'd both done most things right. However, the key difference was that our team had applied the law of momentum, whereas they had not.

The law of momentum encourages people to make quick or immediate decisions and create what I call a *conspiracy to succeed*.

When I was a sales trainer for a training organisation, one of the best things I learned about sales came not from my course material, but from a remarkable 78-year-old woman who did the company's customer relations and outbound sales.

She said to me, "Daniel, when communicating with customers, the one rule you have to follow is always use a comma, never a period."

She shared with me how in every conversation she had, she made sure that at the end of the conversation she'd created some reason to continue it. I thought a lot about this.

In terms of the psychology of decision making, this makes sense. She was creating an opportunity for a continued relationship, as well as engaging the spirit of curiosity.

Think about any TV series you've watched. Does it neatly wrap up every plot line at the end of each episode? Obviously, that strategy would be disastrous for its ratings. So, what does it do? It ends on a cliff-hanger. Cliff-hangers are an example of using a comma not a period.

## Conspire to succeed

So how does this apply to the world of pitching?

First, you need to ask for what you want. It surprises me that very few people are in the habit of asking for what they want. And if you fail to ask for what you want, your chances of getting what you want are low to zero.

Near the end of an investment pitch, say, "Based on the presentation you've seen, we are asking for a valuation of $x$ dollars for $y$ percent in our company. We will use this money to do $a$, $b$ and $c$."

Near the end of a customer presentation, say, "The next steps I see us taking together are $a$, $b$ and $c$."

Near the end of a job interview, say, "From the experience I've had in this interview, I'd like us to continue to a second interview if that's your wish too. Where do you see things progressing from here?

Near the end of a date, say, "I've had a great time with you. I'd love to do this again."

And if it's due diligence, say a little more, but keep the same language structure, such as, "I'm happy that you see value in progressing due diligence. We certainly do too. From here, here's how I see things progressing. You'll be wanting $x$, $y$ and $z$ from us. I see us getting those documents to you by Friday and you spending the next $x$ weeks working through them and asking us follow-up questions. If you need more time, let us know. My intention is not to rush either you or us, but to operate efficiently so we can maintain momentum and focus. Does that sound like a reasonable amount of time to you?"

The quote above was the piece of language that allowed us to progress quickly through due diligence, whereas the other company got stuck. The reason this language works is that it does two critical things at once.

1. It demonstrates leadership of the sales process.

2. It creates clarity about timing for everyone.

It's important to take leadership of the sales process, because doing so shows you in the best possible light. The other party is far more likely to invest in you or buy your product if they can see you taking leadership from the start.

Gaining clarity about time upfront will enhance the likelihood of reaching a decision in the shortest time possible and allows any obstacles to come out so they can be mitigated upfront.

By taking this approach you are selling yourself as a leader, a person who does not wait for other people to set the agenda, but a person who sets the agenda.

If you fail to set the agenda, the customer or investor assumes you will continue not to take leadership throughout their relationship with you. This causes a potential investor to infer that you and they would suffer long sales cycles, and a prospective customer to infer that you and they would suffer long project implementation cycles. In both cases, you both lose.

Our second-round capital raising at Helix8 took less than three weeks between the time we gave our pitch and when we received the investment money in our bank account.

The well-meaning advisors told us that such a time frame was impossible. Yet what they were really saying was that it was impossible *for them*, because they did not want to have simple, direct conversations. During due diligence, I described the length of time I believed it would need for a decision to be realized. I told everyone the conditions that we were and were not prepared to accept for shares and the price range we were prepared to accept.

I am not a naturally direct communicator. My natural style is the opposite of direct, so I had to get over a fear they might think I was being too bold or direct. Yet, the opposite was true. It gave everyone confidence that I could have the discussions that mattered about the things that mattered at the time they mattered.

# Questions

- How can you show leadership from the outset, during and at the end of any decision-making cycle, and in doing so shorten the cycle and inspire confidence in you?

- Are you clear on what you want and therefore what you are going to ask for?

- Have you practiced asking for this out loud and to other people before asking it of your real audience?

- When you ask for what you want, do you do anything that breaks momentum by creating doubt in the other person, such as avoiding eye contact at the last minute or wavering in your tone?

- Are you comfortable taking leadership in a conversation, or do you have limiting beliefs about this being pushy, even though this is what gives others confidence in you?

- Are you creating excuses to opt out of this stage of the tactical element of pitching? If you are, I assure you that when you lose your pitch, you can look back to this as the reason.

Success in pitching is less about how much time you take, and more about many bold moves you make.

# CHAPTER 8

# Bold Moves

If it were not for the tactical dimension of pitching, Helix8 would never have gained investment. Two weeks out from when our first investment arrived, we had succeeded in getting one investor to invest, but others were reluctant to commit. This had never been done in New Zealand, after all. Our lead investor suggested that he be the one to help the others across the line, since as a fellow investor, he had more credibility with them. The tactic worked and the rest is history.

There have been several occasions during a pitch where one bold move has changed everything, either for a client or me. Harvey's tactical pitch over the phone to me as the CEO of Helix8 was 80 percent bold move, 20 percent anticipation.

## Be smart not slow

Here's another example of how to apply the bold move principle.

A few years ago, I was asked by a small company with about 200 staff to help them win an all-important pitch. It was all-important because they'd lost the past three pitches in a row. Because of that, their company was in danger of having to shed staff, which put them in danger of losing their reputation. That meant they were at risk in the future of having to recruit a different type of person, someone who did the grunt work rather than the imaginative work they dreamed of doing.

Through our partnership, they won their next pitch. As with Harvey winning a position at our company, they won their pitch largely due to one seven-minute bold move.

Near the start of our work together, I surveyed the people in the room, who were slightly downcast because of their previous losses. To help change the mood, I asked a tactical question.

"Who knows someone on the panel who's going to judge us?" Lance, an older man and one of the company directors, raised his hand.

I said, "That's great. Who is that person, Lance?" He told me. It turned out he knew the person reasonably well. I said, "Great, have you or anyone else here contacted him?"

Lance objected. "The request for proposal document says that under no circumstance should anyone on the pitch panel be contacted for fear of disqualification."

I had anticipated this objection, so immediately read the following phrase from a report I had brought with me. "It's a mistake to simply assume that your team cannot meet others within the prospect's organisation ... We have done so, more than once, to discover that the clause covering access was not considered important and limited contact was allowed." – RogenSi White Paper (2012) *Winning when times are tough.*

Emboldened by my evidence Lance asked tentatively, "So do you think we should contact that person?" To which I replied, "Do you want to win this pitch?"

He smiled and I said, "I want you to call him now, and here's what I want you to ask him. 'Don, I have a question for you – more of a confirmation really. When we present to you, we want to make sure we hit all the things you care about first time, so you don't have to waste time asking extra questions. So, I want to be clear on the criteria we're going to be judged on. We believe it will be $x$, $y$ and $z$, in that order. Is that correct?'"

I asked Lance whether he felt comfortable with that. He said he did and left the room. A few minutes later he came back. He was barely able to conceal his smile.

He showed me his mobile phone. The call had taken seven minutes and 33 seconds. He said, "Daniel that seven minutes and 33 seconds turned out to be a pretty valuable conversation."

That was Lance's understated way of saying, "That one call was the difference between us being off track and on track to winning the pitch." Lance had asked the question exactly as I'd suggested and he'd been told, "Yes, talk about *x* and talk about *z*, but don't talk about *y*, we don't really care about that so much. But you also might want to talk about *a*, and I'd suggest that the order of importance is *z*, *a*, *x*."

So, in one bold move that took seven minutes and 33 seconds Lance had learned that:

1. We were going to talk about something that wasn't that relevant to them.

2. We were going to miss something that was critically important to them.

3. We were about to spend too much time on one thing and too little time on another.

The lesson is that one bold question, one timely phone call or one well-framed question can be, and often is, the difference between winning or losing. One bold move can overcome hours, weeks or sometimes months of hard toil.

When we won the pitch, the managing director of the company, Joe, asked if he could take me out for lunch. He was normally a reserved man, but I'd never seen him so happy as he was that day. In fact, he was almost embarrassed about the difference that pitch made to his company's success. The win had given them enough new revenue to meet their financial projections for the entire year. He apologized to me that he wouldn't need to use me on pitches for some time, as now their "biggest problem was capacity – not sales."

True to his word, it was two years before he contacted me again. They won that pitch too.

# Questions

- What bold moves can you take to increase your tactical likelihood of winning your next pitch?

- Who can you speak to that you haven't yet spoken to?

- Who can you contact that you haven't yet because you assume they will say *no* to you, forgetting that any question not asked is an automatic 'no' by default?

- How can you be cheekier in what you ask for, more direct about what you want, more able to combine boldness with friendliness, so that the *other* party wants to be part of *your* party?

Just seven minutes of
bold action can undo years
of underperformance.

DELIVERY

While it is true that a great actor will struggle to breathe life into a poor script, it is equally if not more true that a great script can be destroyed by a weak performance. Such is the importance of delivery.

Many researchers have shown the critical importance that delivery plays in creating impact and influence. A movie that does not have good performances and a good script will not be well received. Similarly, a pitch that does not have a good delivery and a good message will be unlikely to receive a 'yes'.

Any conjecture about whether delivery or message is more important misses the point. It's a meaningless theoretical debate that has no relevance to the person who seeks to win pitch after pitch. The simple fact is that both are critically important, and if you fail to do a good job of just one of them, you won't succeed.

Delivery traditionally gets less attention than message. This lack of attention should not be mistaken for a lack of importance. Remember, people decide emotionally, but defend their position rationally.

That means it is unlikely that anyone you pitch to will give as a reason for their 'no', that, "Your body language didn't make me feel confident in you." They will be much more likely to say, "You didn't provide good answers to $x$, $y$ and $z$ in your message."

While message engages the intellect and the emotions, delivery engages solely at an emotional level. Because people decide emotionally, disregard the fact that your audience is unlikely to cite your delivery as a reason for their 'yes' or 'no' and take time to focus on making this aspect of the pitch powerful.

There are many delivery adjustments that matter little to the number of pitches you win. But there are four delivery adjustments that will make a big impact on the number of pitches you win, and therefore a big impact on your life. They are the four adjustments you are about to read about in this section.

CHAPTER 9

# Energy

Energy is the subtlest aspect of the four factors of delivery. Arguably, it is also the most powerful. While the other three aspects – physicality, tonality and pause – are relevant *during* your pitch, energy is what you need to attend to *before* your pitch. The other factors are about what you *do*. Energy is about how you *be*.

Most people expend effort preparing their *message*, but fail to prepare *themselves* for the most important pitches of their lives. It's important to prepare yourself by raising your energy levels, because a cup can only contain a cup-sized volume of fluid. You need to create a larger source of energy, so you don't run out of it too soon to be successful with your pitch. By increasing your energy, the container of influence you can draw from goes from the size of a cup to that of a bucket.

By increasing your energy levels, you increase your capacity for greater boldness of message and greater power in your delivery. Having great command of tonality, physicality and pause, but not taking care of your energy levels is like having a smartphone with a drained battery – a tremendous waste of potential. Think of how you become more constrained with your phone usage when it's only got 10 percent of its battery left. That's how constrained you'll be with your energy when you pitch without recharging your energy in advance.

By attending to energy, your battery gains almost infinite capacity to deliver any level of power you demand of it through your tonality, physicality and pause. Energy is the volume control that allows these other three factors to reach their maximum potential.

Because people decide emotionally but defend their decision

To have your audience say 'yes', they must be emotionally involved; to be emotionally involved, they must be energized, and for them to be energized, you must be energized.

logically, your energy level is key. If people are not energized by what they see, they won't be emotionally involved in what they experience. If they are not emotionally involved in what they experience, they cannot decide to say 'yes' to your pitch.

Being highly energized doesn't mean you need to move around the stage like Anthony Robbins, although that is one option open to you. It can equally mean power under restraint.

Think of it this way. The best hi-fi amplifiers have incredibly high wattage (power) even though they seldom, if ever, are required to use this power. However, their potential power means that under smaller volume commands they can achieve a clearer pitch and purer tones.

In the same way, having greater energy means you can give a clearer pitch with purer tones. You will also have the potential at key moments to give people a taste of the power within you. You can express this power through any of the following:

- raising the volume of your voice

- a poignant pause

- a moment of intense physicality, for example, a bold gesture of leadership such as clapping together your hands or firm placement of one hand on a table.

For these moves to look and feel easy and effortless, your core energy must be high. Otherwise, like a cheap amplifier asked to play music loudly, you'll sound strained or artificial.

## Be an exemplar

So how do you create this high energy? This comes down to two things – morning rituals and role modeling.

It is impossible to have strong physicality on stage if you are not physically fit. Similarly, it is impossible to encourage others to make good decisions with a clear head, if you are not decisive and clear headed. This means that each day, part of raising your energy levels should include some form of physical activity and some form of mindfulness activity.

The physical activity could be anything from running, swimming, yoga, dancing, competitive sport, jumping jacks or Pilates, to any physical activity that you enjoy.

The mindfulness activity could be meditation, prayer or another devotional practice, breathing exercises or a combination of these. Your mindfulness exercise will focus your mind, clear your thoughts and sharpen your decision-making power. It will ensure that you do not lose mental and emotional energy sifting through clutter in your own head when you try to conceive thoughts or vocalize words.

Your mindfulness exercise will also enhance your ability to stay unattached. You will be calmer and more grounded. This gives other people confidence that your energy is solid and grounded, and it helps de-risk the part of the pitch they see as most important and therefore most risky – *you*.

The second component of energy is that you are a living exemplar of the message you deliver. The best way to *appear* bold is to *be* bold. To be bold, you must be taking actions on a regular basis that exhibit boldness.

Chapter 8: Bold Moves goes into detail about how to do this. The key question to ask yourself daily is, "What action should I take today to advance me the most toward my goals?"

The needle-moving activities will typically be the activities that require greater boldness. By taking bold actions regularly, boldness becomes a part of your identity. Because it is a part of your identity, this same boldness will be evident to others in your delivery. Because boldness will be evident in your delivery, your audience will be more energized by what you say and more confident in the recommendations you make.

# Questions

- What are you committed to doing daily to increase your energy, both in terms of your fitness and your mindfulness?

- What actions can you take to better model courage and bold action when you deliver your pitch and ask others to take bold action?

- What is the cost of not implementing this one thing due to a limiting belief that you are not a disciplined person or that you can get away with not doing it?

- Do you want to pitch as though you are a smartphone with only 10 percent of its power left or would you rather keep yourself fully charged so that all your power is available to be used and enjoyed?

CHAPTER 10

# Pause

If you fail to pause, you fail to inspire. That's because decisions are not made while you're speaking, they're made while you're pausing. That means by not pausing, you are not allowing time for the making of decisions.

Here's why decision making can't happen if you don't pause.

As you will recall if you are of a certain age, before the digital camera was the analogue camera. Inside the analogue camera was a film. You had to wind on that film manually after taking each photo. If you took another photo without winding on the film, you got what was called a double exposure, two images on the same piece of film.

Failing to wind on the camera is to analogue photography what failure to pause is to influence – a disaster. Failure to pause causes the listener to try to do two things at once:

- take on what you've just said
- listen to what you are now saying

The human brain isn't good at doing two things at once. When you don't pause, you force your listener to choose between taking on what you've said and listening to what you are saying.

That's a poor choice to ask someone to make when you are trying to influence them. To avoid asking them to make that decision, the solution is simple – pause.

The pause represents the moment where you wind on the film of that old analogue camera. While you pause, they take on what you just said. Then they have clear space for the next thing. They can attend to what you're about to say. Meanwhile, you get to think about what you want to convey next and how best to frame it. The result is that two separate and well-formed pictures take shape in the mind of the person you want to influence.

Pausing is not a stylistic optional extra, but an essential element of pitching. It's also true that the more you pause, the more impact you create. Here's why.

Think of the greatest orators of our time. If you have not already done so, listen to Martin Luther King's "I have a dream" speech. Pay attention particularly to the opening 90 seconds.

Ten years ago, in the first workshop I ran on pitching, I gave people a transcript of the opening segment of this talk and asked participants to read it out aloud.

They took between 27 and 49 seconds. I then said, "This is oratory, and during oratory, a slower pace is more influential. Read it again, this time taking as many pauses as you think a great orator would take."

This time, their times ranged from 33 to 58 seconds. Then I told them that Martin Luther King took 90 seconds to say those same words. They were stunned. Then I showed them Martin Luther King speaking those words. They suddenly understood the power of pausing and a slower pace.

This group was typical. They spoke at roughly twice the pace of Martin Luther King, even after being prompted to slow down.

Most people I work with on delivery believe that impact is created by conveying more information in the same amount of time. They are often shocked to find out that their pace is having the opposite effect on people.

## Create space to inspire

When it comes to influence, the measure of effectiveness is not *how much you've said*, but *how much they have retained*.

When you are comfortable with long pauses, you automatically place yourself in your audience's eyes in the same basket as great inspirational orators such as Martin Luther King. This is not a bad neuro-associative basket to be in, having made only one delivery adjustment.

But the benefits of pausing go beyond neuro-linguistic association and giving people time to reflect on the significance of what you've said. Pausing also gives you time to think about what you're going to say next. This is vitally important.

Without giving yourself time to reflect on what you are going to say next, you must either memorize what you say, something I don't generally recommend, or think about what you're going to say as you say it. This is again a poor choice to have to make.

In terms of the former, I don't recommend memorizing what you're going to say unless you can dedicate as much time to bringing the script to life as an actor does. If you don't, all your effort will go into memorization, and little effort will be left for bringing what you want to say to life. The result is that you will look stilted.

And in terms of the latter, if you're thinking about what you're going to say as you say it, you don't have time to collect your thoughts or your words. This increases the probability that you will make poor word choices.

Failure to pause also makes it more likely that your communication will come from your head not your heart, because you need to use your head to think about what you are saying, rather than *feeling* your way into what you say as you say it.

Your audience cannot say 'yes' to you unless they feel an emotional response to what you say. What are their chances of doing this if you haven't spoken from your own feelings? Remote. So, pausing increases the chance you will connect with your emotions and speak from them.

A side benefit of pausing is that it eliminates most of what I call linguistic junk candy. There are three types of junk candy:

- non-words, such as 'um's and 'ah's

- filler words and phrases, such as 'like', 'you know', 'sort of', 'kind of' and 'I guess'

- restarting sentences or repeating part of a sentence.

This linguistic junk candy has the impact of flashing an imaginary neon light above your head broadcasting that, "I'm not confident in myself and what I'm saying and neither should you be."

So, if pausing is so effective in inspiring others why don't more people do it? Well, firstly, I don't know if anyone has done a great pitch before now on why pausing is a critical rather than an optional extra.

Secondly, you may have a limiting belief around pausing. Have you heard the expression 'an awkward pause'? You may unconsciously assume that pauses are awkward. You may feel uncomfortable about what might be going through your audience's heads as you pause. You may have scripts running through your head, such as, "What's that person thinking of me? Are they looking at me? Are they wondering if I've forgotten what I'm saying?"

They will be thinking none of these things. Your audience really doesn't care that much about you, what they care about is their *experience of you* in what you have said. Most likely they'll be grateful that you've paused long enough for them to take in what you just said. It also gives them time to feel the poignancy of what you've said, because you can also create 'a poignant pause.'

What decides whether a pause is awkward or poignant? You do. If you feel awkward while you pause, then other people will feel awkward watching you being awkward while you're paused. If you feel poignant while you are pausing, then other people will feel the poignancy in your pause and in what you are saying.

I found this out accidentally on 28 December 2005. I was giving my first keynote talk when the unthinkable happened. Halfway through, I forgot what my next point was. "No worry," I said to myself. "This has happened before, I know what to do. In these situations, take a deep breath, engage eye contact with the audience, stand confidently and you'll recollect exactly what you have to say."

I did this. I looked at the audience. I did not recollect what I was going to say. I reflected to myself a second time. "Well, I am talking to a group that's twice as large as any I've talked to before, perhaps I need to take two breaths to account for the larger audience."

I breathed in. I breathed out. I kept looking at my audience. I did not recollect what I was going to say. After a full 20 seconds of pausing I finally remembered what I had to say next. Needless to say, that 20 seconds felt like a whole lot longer to me.

At the end of the talk, people came up, thanked me for my talk and shared how it inspired them. By the third person, I had noticed a pattern. Each person without fail commented on that middle part of my talk. They said, "Your talk was great, but that part in the middle of your talk when you paused for what seemed like an eternity was so poignant, so powerful. And what you said next I will remember for the rest of my life. Thank you."

I was left thinking, "So the part of my talk everyone liked best was the part I did completely by accident?" I went away and when I was next by myself I wrote down in my journal, as I always do after a pitch, one win and one learn. The win? Pause longer more often.

J. S. Bach said, "Music is what happens between the notes." I've come to believe that influence is what happens between the words.

Inspiration means to breathe in. This is significant, because when we are breathing in, we are not talking. That means that inspiration *literally* happens *when you are not talking*. Inspiration happens on the in-breath, while you are pausing.

Listening to yourself pitch will show you whether you're pausing for long enough. Did you know that when you talk your heartbeat will typically beat a little faster? This means your tendency will be to pause for less time. So, when you think you are pausing for long enough, chances are you're not.

## Questions

- What limiting beliefs do you need to shift to feel comfortable with pausing? When would you like to shift these beliefs?

- Do you record every pitch you give? If not, why not? If you do record your pitches, do you listen for your pauses as well as your words?

- How can you practice pausing so that the next time you pitch this behavior is automatic?

- Who 'um's and 'ah's a lot? Who pauses between what they say? What is the impact of each of these people on you?

- Who comes across as more authoritative and influential and more likely to have you say 'yes' to whatever they pitch to you?

Failing to pause means
failing to inspire.

# CHAPTER 11

# Tonality

Tonality was once my Achilles heel. In my previous life as an actor, I got quirky television commercials that relied on physical humor, but not serious speaking parts.

Years later I realized why – my voice simply did not convey a lot of interest or emotion. I managed to get away with this when pitching to a crowd because I could lift the energy enough to compensate for my inexpressive tone. However, in one-on-one pitching conversations where I couldn't justify the same performance energy, my results suffered because my voice remained toneless.

When you're leading an organisation, or any team, you're pitching all the time. My lack of tone undermined my leadership authority, which meant that I was questioned a lot more by my team, co-founders and board.

The missing expressiveness and authority in my tone also meant I had to rely on argumentation to make a case. And as it turns out, using logic to persuade people is far less effective than making bold declarations with an authoritative voice!

## Use tone for impact

Off-Broadway New York actor Peter Rogen understood the power of tonality and physicality. In 1968, between shows, he earned his living helping advertising executives win pitches, substantially improving the success rate of the firms that hired him.

The three-day training course he developed included exercises to improve tonality and physicality, and the company he established with Neil Flett grew into 13 international offices before being purchased by Nasdaq-listed TeleTech in 2014.

I believe that part of Peter Rogen's success was the application of the Bruce Lee principle. He took techniques he'd learned in the world of acting and applied them to the world of business. I'm sure he observed that business executives had only a fraction of the presence that his actor peers had on stage, and thought, "If they had even a bit more presence, they'd win a whole lot more pitches." Years later, I observed the same thing. As an actor, my not-very-expressive voice stopped me getting work. However, in the world of business, my voice wasn't that bad compared to other executives. When giving pitches, I had enough enthusiasm in my voice to create engagement and influence.

There are three key ways to use tonality to influence people.

## 1. Vary your voice to improve your body language

Tonality influences physiology. There's an exercise that's been used for years in presentation skills workshops called the enthusiasm/non-enthusiasm exercise. People get into pairs and each takes a turn delivering a short monologue. In the first monologue, one person talks about something they are passionate about. This could be a hobby, an idea, a cause or a project. The catch is that they must speak in a monotone, removing all enthusiasm from their voice.

In the second round, the other person does the opposite. They talk about a mundane subject they feel ambivalent about, for example, a household chore such as vacuum cleaning or dusting, or an inanimate object such as a chair or whiteboard marker. The catch is that this person must speak with great enthusiasm and passion as though this was the most interesting subject in the world.

When participants debrief, we invariably find the same phenomenon. It was far more engaging listening to the mundane topic talked about with passion, than the passion topic expressed with ambivalence.

In fact, the impact is so pronounced that on many occasions the person speaking on the mundane topic even reports that their faked enthusiasm has convinced them their subject really was interesting.

Their decision to use an enthusiastic tone had not only helped to influence the other person, it had influenced themselves. While the outcome of this exercise is unsurprising, its significance should not be lost. This exercise proves that when it comes to creating impact and influencing people, the tonality we use is more important than the content.

But what do we generally rely on to create an influential message? Don't most people spend their time putting together slides and practicing the content of their message, but very little time practicing the tonality they use to convey their message?

This exercise shows that you would be better placed spending at least some of that time practicing the tone with which you convey your message. The benefit of doing this is pronounced – you will have a more persuasive impact on those you speak to.

But there is another outcome with this exercise. People report that the moment their tonality becomes more engaging, so does their physicality. They gesture more expressively, their face becomes more animated, they use more eye contact and, in some cases, they even start to move around the room.

This side effect communicates a critical point. Physicality and tonality are linked.

If you are new to the idea of using physicality and tonality to become more influential, this is good news for you. What it means is that you can choose to focus on either one, knowing that the other will follow.

If you choose to use a more expressive voice, your physicality will automatically become more expressive too. Similarly, by choosing more expressive physicality such as greater use of gesture, movement and stage presence, your tonality will become more expressive to match.

In one pitching workshop, I asked people to talk in an expressive voice while sitting on their hands. People found it almost impossible. One participant captured the mood of the room when he said, "My hands just wanted to fly out from under me."

Choose physicality or tonality as your starting point knowing that the other will be influenced automatically.

### 2. Extend your tonality by recording yourself

Years ago, during my time as CEO of Helix8, I was interviewed by a researcher into entrepreneurship. It was while listening to the recording of that interview that I noticed how expressive the interviewer's voice was and how inexpressive mine was. This moment of uncomfortable self-awareness was the start of my journey to improve my tonality.

Since what gets recorded gets rewarded, I began practicing my vocal expressiveness while recording myself, each time making a conscious effort to have a more expressive voice. But something strange happened when I listened to myself. I found that however expressive I thought I was being, when I heard myself back it was as if someone had squeezed all the tonality out of my voice.

When I recorded myself on video, I noticed something else – the same was true for my physicality. I thought I'd been moving in an interesting way physically. Yet when I saw myself on video, I looked slightly immobile. There was far more opportunity to use my physicality in an interesting way than I had imagined.

And then I noticed a third thing. Even though I'd been consciously attempting to pause more, when I listened to and watched my recordings I noticed that I could have paused for a whole lot longer. When I conducted workshops, I noticed the same phenomenon in other people. Why was all this occurring?

Then the 'aha' moment dawned. I believe that many people, including myself, have developed a self-monitoring reflex to make sure we are not being too theatrical, for fear of appearing over-the-top, inappropriately comedic or overly animated. This fear leads us to truncate our pauses, rein in our vocal expressiveness and dampen down our physical expression.

While it seems useful to self-monitor around not being too theatrical, the problem is that our response to this urge is about four to five times too strong. We over-respond to this fear of being over-the-top. This over-response dampens down three of the four most critical aspects of delivery, three of the four things that would enable us to influence others – physicality, tonality and pause.

The solution? Conscious overextension and review.

In workshops these days, I give people the license to consciously use tonality, gesture and pause to a degree that they feel is over-the-top. When we watch the video recordings of them afterwards, they are amazed to find that not only was their presentation not over-the-top, but that they could have taken it even further in all three dimensions.

The video feedback gives people confidence to push things further and further. The result is a level of life in their pitch that without this over-extension they would never have given themselves permission to exhibit.

If you are serious about improving your delivery, do two things:

- commit right now to the habit of conscious over-extension and review

- record yourself saying anything at all using tonality, physicality and pause to a much greater degree than you would normally.

### 3. Focus on one thing

There are three major elements you can use to convey greater levels of authority and influence. These are:

- volume

- pitch

- speed.

If you do nothing else to improve your tonality, do this one thing – find the key elements of your pitch, the important ones that you cannot leave to chance as to whether people will remember them.

You'll probably find three to four of these moments. You may also find one key message that you repeat at least twice.

Next, ask yourself the question, "How can I use volume, pitch or speed to make these points more memorable?" That's it.

I suggest you practice a couple of times until it feels natural and then trust that this one adjustment will get your key points remembered, because your audience will recall the emotion you conveyed during those key points by using volume, pitch and speed.

I was recently asked to speak to a group of 150 youth leaders. This was a pitch. The objective was not to win investment, but to win the hearts and minds of our country's future leaders. The best measure of whether you achieve this is a standing ovation.

During the talk I pitched my belief that the All Blacks did not just represent New Zealand's sporting potential, but our potential in any field we applied ourselves to. The talk was emotional, and included looking at the painful cost to the whole country of not pitching our innovation well.

I wanted to end on a powerful positive note. So, I used rhetoric to help do this. But the rhetoric would have been wasted without a shift in tone. I also increased the volume, emphasis and pitch of my voice so it felt like the crescendo of an orchestra as I said the following.

"In this future, we look not to only our landscape for pride, but to our people. In this future, we don't just watch others take the field, we take the field. In this future, our example inspires our children that they can do anything globally.

"In this future, we will rise up and truly have our praises heard afar on every field we take to – fulfilling our destiny as a nation of people who were not content to only conceive, but who reached out and achieved."

The result was a standing ovation.

## Questions

- What are the most important messages in your talk?

- How can you use volume, pitch and speed, combined with pause, to make these moments stand out and have strong emotions anchored to them?

- Are you committed to recording every single pitch you give so you can get the reward of learning from that?

- Who can give you honest instructive feedback about your voice so you can make small adjustments that will mean you have greater impact?

- Next time you pitch, will you simply practice the persuasiveness of your message or also practice the persuasiveness of your tonality?

If eyes are the windows to the soul, then eye contact with your audience is the window to the soul of your pitch.

# CHAPTER 12

# Physicality

As you've just seen, physicality and tonality are closely linked. Make your tonality more expressive and your physiology will follow. Similarly, make your physiology more expressive and your tonality will follow.

Being more expressive makes you more persuasive. The studies on this reveal the same thing consistently – people who command strong physicality and tonality command strong influence.

## Convey your story with your body

When it comes to physicality there are five aspects to work with:

- gesture
- posture
- facial expression
- eye contact
- movement.

Most articles and books I've read on the subject include eye contact in the same category as facial expression, but I've separated it out because it's so important it needs its own category. Also, eye contact is less about facial expression and more about how you relate to your audience. Put another way, it's less about *face* than *interface*.

In this section, we'll be looking at three facets of physicality that make the biggest difference to the level of influence you hold. None of these tools are about using contrived body language or movement during a pitch. They are about subtle adjustments you can make before and during a pitch.

In terms of working with the five aspects of physicality, these are the three facets that I have found to have the greatest influence on the persuasiveness of a pitch.

## 1. The right way to use eye contact

It's impossible to examine this without looking at one of the most commonly used props of the modern era, the PowerPoint presentation. I classify the PowerPoint presentation as a prop because it's a visual add-on intended to *enhance* the message, yet most people use it to *replace* the message. You'll hear more about that later.

Let's first look at some of the traps that most people using PowerPoint fall into. The most common and destructive behavior pattern is looking at the PowerPoint slides when speaking. This conveys two things:

- "I'm more interested in my slides than you."

- "I haven't made any effort to learn the structure of my talk or embody what I'm talking to you about."

In pitching workshops, I model two versions of using PowerPoint. In the first version, I do what most people pitching do – consistently turn my back to the audience, break eye contact and talk while looking at the screen.

In the next version, I once again occasionally turn my back to the audience and look at the screen. However, I make one small adjustment. I pause while turned to the screen, then return my gaze to the audience *before* I resume speaking.

When I ask participants for their response to each example, they say that in the first case it looked as though the presenter was disengaged and therefore they felt disengaged. In the second version, they felt more engaged.

They've also reported that, "It was as if the energy of the presentation was carried through the eyes of the presenter." They were right. This is exactly what is happening.

So, the first rule of eye contact is that while you may look at the screen, don't look at it while speaking. Instead turn to the screen, pause, turn back and speak.

The next rule of eye contact, which is harder to master than it may sound, but is incredibly powerful, is the rule of 'one sentence, one person'. In other words, make eye contact with one person and give them one full sentence, choose another person, look at them and utter another sentence.

What typically happens is that people either scan the audience looking at many people within one sentence, or else they look at one person for most of the sentence then look away just before they finish it.

Again, I model these three different styles to the group and ask for feedback as to the impact on them as an audience member.

In the first version, the constant flitting of eyes from one person to the other gave participants the impression that I was nervous, scattered in my focus and not relating to my audience. Not a great impression to make if you want someone to have confidence in you and your ideas.

In the second iteration, I held my gaze on one person for most of a sentence, but looked away just before the end, before fixing my gaze on another person. The people whose gaze I'd fixed on for most of the sentence but not all of it, repeatedly fed back that they felt deprived of the *impact* of my sentence. They felt as though I had abandoned them early and they therefore didn't take on board the full impact of the statement I had made.

When I ran the same exercise with the one addition of holding my gaze for a moment longer until the sentence finished before turning away, the difference was striking. Participants could remember the statements vividly, they felt the impact of them and they even reported that they felt that I cared for them more.

These subtle differences in eye contact led to pronounced differences in impression. So, make these two adjustments to eye contact and the level of connection your audience experiences with you will go up immeasurably. The result will be that they feel as though you care about them, they remember more of what you say and they experience you as a more confident and focused person.

## 2. The right way to use props

PowerPoint is the most commonly used prop. When people use it, they often stand to the side of the stage with the PowerPoint on center stage as if they were asking the PowerPoint images to be the main character while they play a bit part.

People do this because they feel uncomfortable pitching and expect that a well-structured PowerPoint presentation with sharp images will mitigate their lack of presence. It doesn't. It's like a movie director putting all the actors off to the periphery of the screen in every scene and having the props in the middle, expecting those props to engage the audience more than the actors.

*People* influence people. Inanimate props can only *extend the influence* of a person who already commands influence. Your Power-Point is an inanimate prop, and you fail to remember this at your peril. The people you're pitching to have come to be influenced by *you*, not your props.

If you feel uncomfortable with being seen by people, the solution is not to abdicate responsibility and delegate center stage to an inanimate prop. The solution is to become a better version of yourself so that you feel more comfortable in your skin and can influence more effectively.

This is not a book on how to use PowerPoint effectively. If you want to learn more about the nuances of that, read Carmine Gallo's *The Presentation Secrets of Steve Jobs: How to be Insanely Great in Front of any Audience* (2010, McGraw Hill).

When using PowerPoint:

1. Don't rely on bullet points to convey your message. People are influenced by stories, not lists. Use a handful of words and images instead.

2. Don't read from the PowerPoint slides or use them as handouts. If your PowerPoint presentation makes complete sense without you, then why are you there? It is a prop to enhance the message that comes from you, which only you can deliver.

3. Have time with nothing on the screen. Often, you can achieve this by hitting the 'B' on your keyboard, or you may prefer to leave some intentionally blank slides. What this does is signal a pause where you can reclaim center stage unencumbered by a competing visual distraction.

PowerPoint is just one of many props you can use in a pitch. Depending on what your product or service is, you may be able to bring your product, or an element of it, onto stage. You may be able to pass it around the audience.

If your product is software you may have to get more inventive with your props, as I was forced to during my third-round capital pitch at Helix8.

I asked myself, "What prop can I use to create more impact in my presentation?"

By asking this question, I became aware that our product had the ability to teach students of bioinformatics, a discipline that combines computer science, molecular biology and statistics. I wondered out loud, "Is there a book called *Bioinformatics for Dummies?*" It turned out there was, so I purchased a copy and brought it to my pitch.

At a key moment of the pitch, I brought it out from under the podium, held it in my left hand, pointed to the book and declared, "Students of molecular biology around the planet are having to teach themselves bioinformatics using this book." I then slammed the book on the table, raised my voice and said, "Using our software, no-one will ever have to read this book again!"

The impact was huge. The bang on the table made people sit up and take note. It was a moment of complete theatricality that was richly rewarded. One prospective investor (who ended up investing) spoke about that being the moment he suddenly saw the true power of our software as a teaching tool, not only a research tool.

It didn't take time to achieve that result. I didn't have to spend several minutes building a case for why our product was a great teaching tool. I'd used one bit of theatricality plus two sentences, speaking with conviction about its value as a teaching tool. Props are a vital element of storytelling, when used responsibly and sparingly.

### 3. The right way to use body language

To make a big difference to the impact you make when you speak, use body language adjustments not only during but before your talk.

Your exercise for this chapter is to visit **www.ted.com** and watch the 20-minute presentation by Amy Cuddy called "Your body language shapes who you are."

This is the second most viewed TED Talk of all time and, based on its rate of new viewers per year, it's on track to become the most watched TED Talk of all time. Why? Because she gives the recipe for the right way to use body language to have greater persuasive impact. Her recipe only takes two minutes and it's based on research.

In her presentation, Cuddy makes a powerful pitch for the practice of spending two minutes before each pitch in a power pose she calls the Wonder Woman position. In this position, you straighten your back, place your feet apart slightly at shoulder width and place your hands on your hips. Then hold this pose for two minutes.

In Cuddy's research, she found that doing high-power poses for two minutes decreased cortisol levels in the body by about 25 percent and increased testosterone levels in the body by about 20 percent. Why is this significant? Because cortisol is a stress hormone and testosterone, which is present in both men and women, is the dynamism hormone.

The most persuasive leader is the one who has that combination of calmness and dynamism. Most leaders are one or the other, dynamic but not calm, or calm but not dynamic. This power pose by itself raises your dynamism by 20 percent and your calmness by 25 percent. That's an impressive transformation from just a two-minute investment.

See in this figure the difference it makes to your ability to influence.

### Leader as Influencer

|  | Not dynamic | Dynamic |
|---|---|---|
| Calm | **Likeable** | **Influencer** |
| Not calm | **Chaotic** | **Boss** |

Since discovering Cuddy's two-minute life hack, I've been routinely using it before each pitch I give. Unlike an actor's voice or physical warm-up techniques, which can only be done in private (otherwise you risk freaking people out), this technique is socially acceptable. I often do it as I'm being introduced and about to go on stage.

## Questions

- Who can you practice holding the 'one sentence, one eye contact' gaze with?

- Can you spare two minutes to make yourself 20 percent more dynamic and 25 percent calmer?

- What props can you use to make your next pitch more powerful?

- By focusing on your tonality has your physicality become more powerful? Or do you notice the opposite – by choosing to extend your gestures just a little bit, is that having an impact on your tone of voice?

MESSAGE

Of the four areas of pitching, message was the one I naturally gravitated to initially. The mathematician in me enjoyed the formula of constructing powerful messages. Since the age of four, I've been fascinated by the structure of language. At university, it was natural that I would study English and, within that, gravitate to researching the areas that had the most practical relevance – narrative, drama and conversational analysis.

My English degree taught me there is no single way to perceive a book but that it can have many interpretations. This helped me understand that there is no single way to receive a product; it can have many different interpretations.

Throughout my twenties, I devoured novels and theatre to satiate my love of language. These days my love of language has been turned to analyzing people's pitches, looking for subtle ways to make the two percent improvement that is the difference between winning and losing.

Before I began using the Bruce Lee approach of synthesizing four traditions to arrive at the simplest, most direct and most powerful result, I started coaching entrepreneurs by concentrating solely on the messaging dimension.

Just by an entrepreneur changing the way they used language in their written material, on their website or in their opening lines of a sales conversation, they typically achieved revenue increases of around 40 percent.

After some time, I realized that their level of improvement would plateau if their message was not accompanied by a powerful delivery, the right mindset and shrewd tactics.

Message was critical, but by itself was not a strong enough lever to create exponential increases in results. Only by combining message with the other three levers covered in this book did tenfold improvements in commercial results regularly occur.

Often when people prepare to pitch, message is the only thing they consider, apart from their PowerPoint slides. However, only through combining message with the other three elements can it became powerful.

Equally, without looking at your message, what you say and the structure and devices you use to say it, you've got nothing.

There are a lot of messaging adjustments that will matter little to the number of pitches you win. But there are four adjustments to your message that will make a big impact on the number of pitches you win, and therefore a big impact on your life. They are the four adjustments you are about to read about in this section.

CHAPTER 13

# Questions

Some of the most phenomenal pitches have led to wins because the pitcher started by asking the right question.

One question I ask business clients is, "How could you sell to 10 times as many people with no more effort?"

The exact words may change, but the essence of the question remains the same. I recently used this sequence of questions with a client, David, the CEO of a high-tech company.

**Question 1:** "It seems to me that you're getting one sale at a time. Who could you talk to so that you could gain multiple sales at one time?" David: "Well, I could be speaking at a conference."

**Question 2:** "Great, what conferences could you be speaking at?" David mentions a couple of conferences.

**Question 3:** "Which of those two do you think would be easiest to get to speak at and of the highest value to you?" David: "Well that would be $x$ conference because I already know the person who organizes it."

**Question 4:** "Is there anything stopping you from ringing up this person right now and asking if you could speak at their conference?" David: "No."

**Question 5:** "Great, well in that case, what could you say to that person so they would see you speaking at their conference as a necessity?" We brainstormed the answer together. And once we had the answer I asked one more question.

**Question 6:** "How could we ask them to introduce you, so that by the time you came on stage to speak your audience was already waiting with bated breath?" David: "Well, I would be introduced as the expert who had a technology that everyone at the conference serious about playing in the digital game should get."

What allowed us to 'play ball at speed' was the combination of the right questions and David's growth mindset.

Within a few months, David had spoken at the conference to more than 500 people. He had been introduced as the expert with the indispensable technology that everyone should get. Because of that, the next day he had a queue at his stand.

When I rang him on the Monday after the conference to debrief, he told me that his biggest problem now was that he had 47 new orders to fill and this had highlighted a bottleneck in his sales fulfilment process.

Another time I asked Bruce, the CEO of another high-tech company, the following questions:

**Question 1:** "What would be the one conversation you could have that would unlock many sales at once?" He replied, "Well, rather than talking to individual basketball associations I could talk to the CEO of Basketball New Zealand."

**Question 2:** "Do you know this person already?"
Bruce: "I do know him, but not well."

**Question 3:** "Do you know about what his strategic objectives as a CEO of Basketball New Zealand are for the next three years?" Bruce: "No."

**Question 4:** "Could you find out?" Bruce: "Absolutely."

**Instruction:** "Great. Here's the tactical bold move I suggest you use. Ring him up and book a meeting, based on what you already understand you can offer him, which is of value. After you've done that, have a second phone call where you say, 'Look, to make the most of our time together during the meeting, I have a few questions to make sure I'm on target with what I say to you. This will take about 10 minutes. Would that be okay?'"

**The result:** Bruce uncovered the three main strategic objectives of the CEO. And based on that, he spoke only of the elements of his product that related directly to how he could meet that CEO's strategic objectives. The meeting was highly successful and, at the time of writing, Bruce had done business deals with five of the eight basketball associations in New Zealand – as a direct result of that one conversation.

On another occasion, I was asked to run a workshop with a company that wasn't winning enough pitches. It turned out that the CEO, members of the senior management team and the sales team were all at the workshop. So, I looked around the room and asked them my first question of the day.

**Question 1:** "Well it looks like we have enough of the right people in this room to make decisions on this very day about how we win business in the future – would you agree?" Leadership team consensus: "Yes."

**Question 2:** "So, to get the most out of today, do you want to come away with ideas or do you want to come away with decisions already implemented that will impact how many tenders you win from as soon as you step out of this room?"

**Leadership team consensus:** "The latter of course."

That simple closed question created the context in which the team agreed to three concrete actions that were immediately implemented. Within weeks, their pitch win rate had increased by more than 40 percent and it has remained at least at that level since.

## Ask the right questions

You can use questions to stimulate people to think in more imaginative ways than that during conversations. The three conversations above were coaching conversations, and every coaching conversation is a pitch, because as a coach you are constantly pitching to your client the value of behavior change.

In presentations, you can use rhetorical questions in a similar way. To put it in comic-book terms, the difference between a question in a conversation and a question in a presentation is that the other person's response is not a speech bubble, it's a thought bubble.

The people in the audience for your presentation will still have a response to your question; they will simply think it rather than speak it. That means a rhetorical question can still guide the imagination of the people listening to your pitch in in very powerful ways.

An example of this is one of the greatest pitches ever given, Winston Churchill's 'We will fight on the beaches' speech. He spoke to the British population at a time when many were expecting him to announce surrender. He pitched that the best course of action was never to surrender but to fight till the bitter end.

Before he gave his pitch, this was neither the most obvious nor the most popular course of action. Yet through his rhetoric, oratory, use of metaphor, story and questions, in one pitch, he turned the tide of public opinion and arguably the tide of the war.

At one point, he asked two powerful rhetorical questions. "Can you conceive a greater objective for the Germans in the air than to make evacuation from these beaches impossible, and to sink all these ships which were displayed almost to the extent of thousands? Could there have been an objective of greater military importance and significance for the whole purpose of the war than this?"

Churchill follows with this statement. "They tried hard, and they were beaten back; they were frustrated in their task."

The previous two rhetorical questions serve as a frame. Had Churchill merely said the Germans were beaten back and they failed, the true significance of this failure would have been lost. His rhetorical questions made it clear that the whole purpose of the war was to do what the British Royal Air Force had thwarted the Germans from doing.

As I referred to above in Chapter 5: Anticipation, another powerful questioning technique is the 'you may be thinking' pattern. I used this language pattern during Helix8's third-round of capital raising when it came time to talk about valuation.

At this point of the pitch, I had already described the milestones our company had achieved since our previous investment round. I then said, "You may be thinking, based on these accomplishments, what valuation premium are we looking for since our last round? Are we looking for a 30 percent, 50 percent or even a 100 percent premium in share price?"

"Well, we're are looking for a 10 percent valuation increment. Because while the milestones have been significant, what's more important is that we get on with the task together as quickly as possible of closing this next investment round and growing the sales of our business. And we don't want valuation to be a question that gets in the way."

Because of this use of questioning to frame the valuation, no one questioned the valuation we were seeking.

If you watch Steve Jobs' product pitches, including the end of the iPhone launch, you will see him use rhetorical questions when it comes to unveiling the price of a new product. The rhetorical question goes as follows.

"Well, based on all this additional capability, how much more should we be charging for this device?" The answer to his rhetorical question is always, of course, "No more, we are charging the same price," as whatever he is comparing the new product to – usually its previous version. Applause resounds and because of the framing question, no one questions price.

You can also use questions to signal transition from one part of your pitch to another in a way that maximizes the empathy from those you pitch to. I use this technique a lot. The way I segue from one part of the pitch to another might go like this:

"So, what problem do we solve?"
"So, why is this problem important?"
"So, what do we do?"
"So, how is our approach different to anyone else's?
"So, what's unique about our team?"
"So, why is the timing right, right now? or "Why is this a wave

that's just about to break, not some white water that's already broken or not some distant hump on the horizon? Here's why."

"So, how are we going to make money from this?"

By using questions to announce each element of the pitch rather than simply stating "Here's our business model", which is boring, expected and unengaging, I put myself inside the mind of the person listening, anticipating and reading their thoughts. This rhetorical questioning technique lets them know unconsciously that I've thought about the questions they will have and the order in which they will have them.

I always pause a little after each question to allow the anticipation and interest to build before I supply the answer (see Chapter 10: Pause).

You've probably noticed that every chapter of this book ends with a list of questions. Why? Without these questions, it's likely that you would just see a bunch of ideas but not ask yourself how to apply them. Including questions is an expression of my intention that you don't just pick up more ideas to not use, but that you implement strategies that cause profoundly positive changes in your life and business.

Each question has been developed to help remove the blocks in the way of you applying the principles in this book. They create a bridge between the book's concepts and the circumstances in your life and business. The reflections sparked off by the questions enable you to construct this bridge.

# Questions

- How can you ask powerful questions to gain more information about your audience before you even start your pitch?

- How can you pitch in such a way that you can gain many sales or investors at one time, rather than only one at a time?

- How can you use rhetorical questions to powerfully guide the imagination of the people who are listening to you?

- What questions can you use to signal the transition from one part of your pitch to another?

- What is the most powerful commitment you can make to yourself right now concerning your use of questions that would transform the level of result you currently enjoy from your pitches?

Lack of clarity creates anxiety.
Anxiety creates evasive action.

CHAPTER 14

# Structure

Once, over a 90-day period, I had an assignment to coach more than 100 of the country's top research scientists on how to pitch. Because of the sheer volume of pitches I saw in a short time, I would have had to be asleep to not notice the patterns that caused some to influence successfully where others didn't.

Many of these success-or-fail moments were due to how people structured and ordered their information. In fact, much of their success was due to what they said, or rather failed to say, *in the opening two minutes.*

By the 12th pitch, I had drafted a formula for what needs to be conveyed in the opening two minutes. By the 36th pitch, I had refined this formula down to three critical elements.

I started coaching the scientists to strictly follow this formula – and suddenly their results went up considerably.

At the end of the first one-day workshop at which I used this formula, one scientist earnestly told me, "I didn't believe that level of change in the impact of one's communication was possible in one day."

After the scientists had delivered their pitches to their investment panel, I was told that not only had they won investment, but that the investment panel was surprised at the quality of message they were hearing.

## Address the key issues

So, what are the three necessary structural elements of a pitch? They are three questions you need to address and that you need to address in this order:

**Question 1:** Why is solving the problem important, and what is it you've got that solves that problem?

**Question 2:** How is what you've got relevantly different to anything else in the world?

**Question 3:** How is your team relevantly unique?

This approach works because it's simple, bold and direct. Traditional pitch techs talk about the importance of describing the problem, your solution, competitive differentiation and the team. However, without nuance, these template approaches to pitching, though well-meaning, are unhelpful.

Firstly, they give you no guidance on how to describe the problem.

Secondly, they provide no guidance on one or two key pieces of language that must be used when describing your difference from competitors.

Thirdly, they don't provide guidance on how to describe your team.

Fourthly, they don't give any importance to when and the order in which these things are addressed.

If these three questions aren't addressed in *the opening two minutes*, it will make someone less likely by an order of magnitude to say 'yes' to you.

You may be thinking, surely that's not possible! It's not only possible, it's essential. If you are struggling to make this possible, it's because you're saying non-essential things, leaving not enough time for you to say what is essential.

You may also be thinking, "Well surely if I miss something, or if I get the order wrong, someone will ask a question later and I can answer it then, right?" Wrong.

If during question time someone asks a key question about your product, they have listened to your entire pitch assuming your product has no real differentiation to anyone else's. That's a low state of inspiration to be listening in.

Let's imagine that at the end of your pitch, a member of your audience asks, "I see how your product is different, but I couldn't see why that difference is so relevant?" Let's imagine that you give the perfect answer and now they are happy. Everything is now all good, right? No. Everything is not all good. They half-listened to your entire pitch with an unanswered question in their head, and consequently, they weakly attended to your information and were weakly influenced by your persuasion.

You may be thinking, "Well, why would someone assume the negative?" The answer is, because it's human nature. It's hardwired into our neurobiology that in the absence of clarity to suspect the worst.

In prehistoric days, if we saw a large slightly out-of-focus shape in the distance, which may or may not be a predator, we couldn't afford to give that creature the benefit of the doubt. We had to assume the worst for the sake of our survival. "This is something that could eat me – take evasive action, now."

This is just as true today as it was in prehistoric times. In the modern world, if your pitch lacks clarity, you create anxiety in your audience leading to the evasive action of avoiding investing or buying or being persuaded by your arguments.

A lack of clarity causes people to run away from a perceived risk so they can return to safety. Saying 'yes' to a pitch when you are unclear on anything is deeply unsafe. So, as the pitcher, your job is not to create eventual clarity, it is to manage the state of your audience so they do not experience, even temporarily, the anxiety that is created by momentary non-clarity.

Unless you explicitly tell people up front why the problem you are solving is important, they will assume the problem you are solving is not important.

Unless you explicitly tell people up front that you have the only product in the world that can do $x$, people will assume that you don't have the only product in the world that can do $x$.

Unless you explicitly tell people that you have the only team in the world that has the combination of skills $a$, $b$ and $c$, your audience will assume that you don't have the only team in the world that can do $a$, $b$ and $c$.

So, why is it so important to describe the problem you solve before you describe your solution? Or as I prefer to put it, why is it so important that you spend about three quarters of your time describing *why* you are relevant before you describe *what* you do?

It's about setting the stage. In a story, characters don't just walk randomly onto the set or into a scene. We need to care about them as or before they walk on. If we don't care about them, we don't engage in the play or movie.

Similarly, to have relevance, you must set the scene for your product as solving a problem. If you don't do this, your product won't be perceived as a hero and your audience won't care about it. As you'll see in Chapter 16: Story, in our third-round capital-raising pitch at Helix8, I set the scene by painting the backdrop of a world in which, due to their clunky cumbersome tools, smart scientists were kneecapped in their ability to do research into diseases that impact the lives of people we care about.

I described the problem before describing the solution we offered. But I didn't stop at describing the problem and nor should you. It's also important to describe the *impact* of the problem.

One research group I worked with had found a way to significantly reduce the occurrence of patient injury from lack of oxygen to the brain during surgery.

Using the formula of describing the problem and then the impact of the problem, they came up with a message that was simple, direct and highly emotive.

Xavier, a research scientist, began by answering Question 1, "Why is solving the problem important and what is it you've got that solves that problem?"

Xavier: "Every year, *x* number of patients around the world wake up from surgery only for they and their surgeons to discover that they have been brain-damaged during the operation because they didn't get enough oxygen."

That's a pretty emotive description of the problem, but we didn't want to stop there. He continued.

"The impact of that problem is devastating. It's devastating to the surgeon who didn't know during the operation that he or she had damaged the patient, and who only finds out afterwards when they ask them to perform a routine action such as lifting a pen and discover they can't. It's devastating to the families of the patient.

And, obviously, it's devastating to the patients themselves.

"It has massive financial repercussions. There are legal and emotional repercussions as well as the obvious physical ones. In many instances, lack of oxygen during surgery can even cause death. "And this is all preventable. Solving this is not easy, but it is possible, and we believe we've found a way to do this."

Notice how the extra effort he made to describe the impact of the problem generated care, not to mention curiosity, from the audience before his solution enters the scene. By now, you're probably rooting for them to have a solution to a problem that a minute ago, you didn't know existed.

Xavier then answered Question 2, "How is what you've got relevantly different?"

"We are the only research group in the world that has found a way to use existing patient intensive care data to unlock patterns that gives surgeons not only clues but answers to the question of what patient data to monitor and what not to monitor during surgery.

"Using that data, we believe we can reduce the chance of a patient not receiving enough oxygen to the brain during surgery to near zero. Addressing this critical area of patient care would solve needless devastation to lives and livelihoods around the world."

Next, he answered Question 3, "How is your team relevantly unique?"

"Not only do we have the only technology that can mine the data for this information using existing data sources, but we have the only team in the world that combines the specific specialist skills required to solve this complex problem."

Xavier's colleague Larry then went on to describe exactly the skills that were required and how they were the only team in the world that had combined these skills into a workable solution.

This pitch was very successful. While the researchers are still in their early days, they now have key stakeholders behind them so they can take this technology to the next level. Xavier and his research team achieved this largely because of their ability to sequence information in the way the human brain needs to receive it to make a decision.

They set the scene, by getting us to care about the situation before they talked about their product. In the original Star Wars movie, Luke Skywalker's line to Princess Leia, "I've come to rescue you", only makes sense because the scenes beforehand tell us that the situation is bad and requires a rescue mission. We have already seen that Princes Leia is a fighter and that she carries the hopes of many, that the enemy has captured her and that her life is in danger. By then, we care about what happens to her.

I've also seen many people lose pitches not because of what they said, but because of the order in which they said it. In pitching it's not only important that the audience knows about Princess Leia. They must also know the consequences (impact) of not saving her – an untimely death, the forces of darkness winning and so on. A pitch needs to be as emotive as possible by describing the impact of non-action, the impact of continuing to live in a world where the solution doesn't exist.

Growth mindset is often weak in sales teams, particularly among salespeople who believe they are pretty good already. At the start of a workshop, I often say, "Today, you can either grow your ego, or you can grow your commercial results. Choose one."

Almost all experienced salespeople claim to be experts at framing a problem before talking about the solution. And yet usually these people fall short when it comes to capturing at an emotional level the impact of the problem they solve before their solution comes charging into the arena.

Their message often sounds like a formulaic script, which not only fails to emotionally engage, it causes me to disengage because it sounds and feels like a sales script, not a story.

A quick coda as to why it's important to address all three questions in the first two minutes. The two-minute idea came from years ago, when I was interviewing Dr Jay Kunin from Tech Coast Angels for a magazine article I was writing on pitching.

He told me he'd just been at a speed pitching competition. I asked him what he'd learned. He said, "Well Daniel, what I learned is the other 13 minutes really don't matter." I said, "Really, Jay?"

He said, "Yes. If you can't describe what you've got in two minutes, you can't describe it in 13 or 15 minutes or any length of time we give you."

Influence is achieved through clarity, not hyperbole.

No matter how long your pitch is, first impressions linger. What you say in the opening two minutes defines whether someone listens passively and intellectually or whether they listen actively and emotionally. In other words, it determines whether they listen in the state from which they are incapable of deciding to say 'yes', or in a state from which they are capable of and likely to say 'yes'.

In the introduction to this book, I made the bold claim that sometimes a single word can be the difference between winning and losing a pitch.

That word is ... 'only'.

Compare the weak claim, "We have the specific specialist skills required to solve this complex problem," with the strong claim, "We have the only team in the world that combines the specific specialist skills required to solve this complex problem."

During the sequence of pitching workshops for research scientists, as any director would, I had them do several takes until they confidently included the word 'only' in their pitch. I then turned to the audience and asked, "Was there a difference?" The consensus answer was, "a massive difference."

We spent some time nuancing the message until the 'only' claim they made was 100 percent true. In pitching, you should never spin. Don't conceal information or use hyperbole to make the status of your product, the caliber of your team or the impact of the problem sound any different to what it is. Spin is the tool of the amateur pitch artist.

Even if you win by manipulating the truth, it is a loss, because the difference between reality and your presentation of reality will quickly emerge, causing stress in the relationship between you and those you pitched to. Quite aside from the stress it will cause you and the credibility it loses you, it's not even the most effective way to influence.

As you can imagine, research scientists have a strong need to make sure that what they say is in alignment with the facts. That's what led them to be scientists. These scientists were relieved when I told them to state their caveats, to reveal the things they weren't yet sure about and to be up-front with the risk of failure in their research.

Not only did they feel better pitching when they were being 100 percent honest, but those hearing the pitch trusted them more, leading to a greater likelihood they would say 'yes' and to a shorter due diligence process.

Back to the word 'only'. Without the word 'only' people assume that some other team somewhere could do or are already doing what you are doing. They assume that some existing product does what your product could do. The word 'only' communicates a level of boldness and certainty, which gives people the confidence to take the next step with those pitching.

You may wonder "how do I know if am the only one?" In this case, you simply say, "To the best of our knowledge, we are the only group that ...."

In pitching workshops, occasionally someone says, "But isn't using the word 'only' egotistical?" The answer is 'no' – providing your intention is good. The key here is that your intention is to use 'only' to provide clarity to your audience about how you are relevantly different, not to beat your chest and say, "I'm better than everyone else."

A single world can change the world. And that word is 'only'.

## Questions

- How can you make your impact more emotional and personal so that you're speaking to the heart of the decision psychology of the people listening to you?

- Do you spend about three quarters of your time describing the problem or have you been placing more emphasis on describing your product or service?

- Have you looked at the structure of your pitch and taken out everything from the first two minutes that doesn't address the three key questions? If not, what is stopping you from doing this?

Create cliffhangers, not completeness.

# CHAPTER 15

# Rhetoric

Rhetoric is the art of using words well when speaking or writing. There are as many rhetorical devices in language as there are different ways to kick in martial arts. And just as there are probably only three types of kick that are effective in a street fight, I believe there are only three types of rhetoric that are essential to learn and apply in pitching. These are:

- framing
- metaphor
- succinctness.

## Set the right frame

Framing is a fantastic way to say something you feel afraid of saying. My first business coach taught me the golden lesson of using framing to have any conversation, when she said, "Daniel, there is no conversation in the world that you can't have so long as you frame it right."

This instilled in me confidence that my previous difficulty in having conversations could be resolved, simply by using the right language frame. Since then, I've had many conversations I might never have had, believing them to be too difficult or challenging. Now I ask myself, "What framing can I use so that this conversation is easy and effortless for both me and the other person?"

Just as a frame around a picture alters our perception of the picture, a frame in our language alters the perception of our words. Just as a visual frame directs a viewer's attention, a frame in language directs the audience's attention to the ideas and thought patterns you want them to share with you.

Recently a client was describing a pitch he needed to make in his personal life. He wanted to find a way to get bridging finance so he could purchase a new property. It became clear that the investor in his company had the financial means to give him that bridging finance, but my client had a reservation about pitching this idea to him. He said, "My investor has done so much already and I've asked so much of him, I feel that asking for one more favor is asking too much."

I said to him, "Well, George, there's no conversation in the world you can't have so long as you frame it right. So how could you frame that conversation so that it's easily and effortlessly had by you and easily received by him?"

He said, "Well, I guess I could express the very thing I'm nervous about. I could just say, 'Hey, this might be a little bit cheeky or forward, and I feel I've already asked so much of you that I wasn't going to ask you this, but then I thought I probably should because it might be something you want to do. I've got this question for you, can I ...'" and George went into the 'ask'.

George had come up with exactly the right frame in a way that felt comfortable to him. And the result was that the investor offered him bridging finance without any awkwardness on either person's part – such is the power of framing.

### Frame No 1: State the thing you fear

The rule here is that when you say what is making you nervous about having a conversation, it takes the power away from it. Doing so shows that you have self-awareness. It also allows you to get on with simply having a conversation in a way where, because of your vulnerability, the other person can see that you're not attached to the outcome. If you had one frame to learn, this would be the one. It can be applied in most situations.

### Frame No 2: Here's why this is great for you

The company director in Chapter 8: Bold Moves, who made the bold move that led to his company winning his multi-million-dollar pitch, made his 'ask' more likely to get a 'yes' by using framing. Had Joe said, "We'd like to verify whether our understanding of your decision-making criteria is correct or not," he may have received a different answer. Instead, he framed his ask by saying, "We want to make sure that we use our pitching time effectively, that we don't say anything irrelevant and that we are on topic, so it's as easy as possible for you to make a decision."

This frame is an example of showing the other party why what's about to be said is going to be in their best interests. Who on a pitching panel doesn't want to hear information from someone who's taken the time and effort to find out whether what they're about to say is relevant?

What Joe effectively said was, "I've placed myself in your shoes and from that standpoint imagined what you'd like to hear and here's what I think it is. I'm not asking you to give away any crown jewels, we've just done some work to imagine what you might want to hear. Can you please verify whether we've got it right or not so our pitch can leave you in the best place to make a decision?"

This frame shows you've thought about the other person's point of view. It works because it makes your empathy and effort to understand their viewpoint explicit and sells the benefit to them of why they should give you the opportunity or information you seek. In this case, Joe benefited them by setting up a more engaging and relevant meeting, something everyone on a pitching panel craves.

**Frame No. 3: The vulnerability frame**

This frame works well in one-on-one conversations, but generally shouldn't be used in presentations, because when presenting you're expected to be the alpha person. In the context of a conversation, the other person is much more likely to forgive any inexperience or imperfections in message or delivery.

In the story that Aki shared with me that I mentioned in Chapter 1: Non-attachment, he used a vulnerability frame. He acknowledged that he'd never sold before and so asked for permission to be imperfect. By doing this, he showed himself to be more authoritative, not less, because he demonstrated that he was comfortable to be himself with his level of experience.

It also took the interaction from a business-to-business interaction to a human-to-human interaction. By deepening the connection to this level, Aki tapped into a deeper form of influence by allowing himself to be perceived as just one imperfect human being speaking to another imperfect human being.

### Frame No 4: It occurred to me that ...

This frame is useful if you want to start communicating in a different way with people you know well. It is the answer to the self-limiting mindset of, "I can't talk differently to that person, it'll be weird or they'll be surprised."

For example, when an organization leader who's not in the habit of finding out the motivations and long-term goals of someone in their team suddenly shows an interest, it can come as a shock to that team member.

The 'it occurred to me that' frame helps gets around this problem, as in the following example.

"Hey Mary, it occurred to me that I've been your team leader for a while now and that I haven't really taken the time to find out what you want in your career. That's an oversight on my part, because I believe the best way to grow a team is to grow the individuals in that team, and you're an important part of this team. But I can't do that unless I know how you want to grow. I don't want to make assumptions, I want to know what you want so that hopefully I can give you more of that."

### Frame No 5: Change is the only constant

In pitching, you are often asking people to change their behavior or their view of the world. The problem here is that humans crave comfort, even if we know that it's not the optimal way to live.

Ollie faced this challenge when he was pitching his idea of personal rapid transport. Even though it sounds superior to existing transport, everyone is used to a world in which cars are the norm. In Chapter 16: Story, you'll see how we used the frame of change as the only constant, combined with the story of the evolution of transport over a 200-year period, to move the audience to readiness to back the next major change in urban transport around the world.

This example shows how when framing is combined with story it can be particularly powerful.

## Use metaphor

Aristotle said that metaphor is the essential tool of every leader. In fact, he went further in his book, *Poetics*, saying, "The greatest thing by far is to have a command of metaphor." While we might want a leader to have a few other tools today, his quote reminds us how important a command of metaphor is to our ability to influence people. After all, the aim of every pitch is to *lead people to a place of new understanding*.

You will have noticed my frequent use of metaphor throughout this book. In fact, this book is an homage to the power of metaphor. If I were to strip out every metaphor, its impact would be greatly reduced.

In the introduction, I used the metaphor of martial arts and Bruce Lee's philosophy of how to make any system of thought work on the streets. I also used the metaphor of the street fight to describe the importance of an approach to pitching that integrates just the key elements from different traditions to create something of relevance in the pitching arena.

To try to convey this data and research would not only have taken longer, it would have lost your attention, therefore being less effective in persuading you of the importance of combining different traditions to develop an effective system of pitching.

### So why is metaphor so effective?

There are two reasons. The first is to do with how we process information. The brain processes every word as a picture. This means that when there are many words, there are a lot of pictures to hold in the brain at one time. Creating a unified picture helps with the task of remembering everything.

This can be done through story or through metaphor. A metaphor creates a visual image that allows us to remember and then quickly make sense of the point being made.

When pitching, one of your tasks is to ask your audience to

use their effort not to understand you, but to *decide to back you.* Because metaphor lowers the effort spent understanding, there is more space left in the minds of your audience to make decisions in your favor.

The second reason metaphor is powerful is efficiency. Often when you're pitching you need to introduce unfamiliar concepts. To get people to understand new concepts from scratch can be a challenge. This is where metaphor is invaluable. You build your metaphor on something those people know already about and add your new concept. By using metaphor, you create a short cut.

For example, to describe the efficiency power of metaphor, I could use the following metaphor. Trying to get people to understand from scratch is like growing a tree from a seed. It takes a long time and people may lose patience waiting for the result. Using a metaphor is like taking an existing tree and simply grafting on a new branch. It takes less time to grow and people are more likely to stick around for it to bear fruit.

In a recent talk to industry leaders, I pitched the idea that, "Our first impulse must be to grow the technology entrepreneur, not to replace them." In it, I used the metaphor of a parent and a child, as follows.

"The founder of a company is the parent and their discovery or innovation is their child. Now, the founder has two out of the three things needed to be successful. They have the product and the product knowledge. The only thing they lack is some of the skill needed to take it further. And because they haven't yet acquired those skills, we make the mistake of thinking we should get rid of them and bring in an external CEO.

"It's a huge mistake. By doing this we have robbed the child – the product – of its birth parent and we've brought in a foster parent. Now, that foster parent may look better on paper, but we know from experience that ninety-nine times out of a hundred, a birth parent will do a better job. And, if we truly believe in that birth parent, any absence of skill can be easily made up with our investment in helping them to grow that skill."

I continued. "Did Bill Gates have all the skills he needed when he started off? What would have happened to the infant company called Microsoft if he'd been replaced early on? What happened to Apple when the birth parent was taken away? And what happened to Apple when the birth parent returned?"

This argument was powerful because no one could deny that, in most cases, a birth parent makes a better parent than a foster one, even if that foster parent looks better on paper. A single metaphor communicated a powerful idea about the impact of love. A parent who fundamentally loves their child will rise to the occasion. They will not be perfect, but they will do a great job in growing their child. And if we help that parent grow, the results for both parent and child will be phenomenal.

## Be succinct

Seven years at university, during which I wrote a thesis, almost destroyed my ability to be succinct with language. The length of my sentences grew. The length of each word grew. My writing eventually became readable only to other academics.

Unfortunately, this style of writing was disastrous when it came to pitching ideas to people outside my immediate circle. It was particularly disastrous in business. It disconnected me from people as they struggled to understand what I was saying. It meant that my audience's effort was spent in understanding me rather than in deciding to back me.

Not only did I use too many long words and sentences, I overloaded my pitches with far too much information because I believed I had to tell the full story. My other belief was that if I said enough stuff, something would stick. This is known as the 'spray and pray' approach to pitching. It is fatally flawed. It doesn't work – for two reasons.

Firstly, spray and pray is like banging away on piano keys, hoping that over enough time some of the notes will be right and create a powerful melody, instead of making the effort to filter out the wrong notes and play only the right notes in the right sequence to create music.

Secondly, when people hear even two back-to-back ideas that they don't understand or don't see as relevant, they quickly stop making an effort to understand you; they stop listening actively and start listening passively. In other words, they stop listening with their emotions engaged.

The moment this happens, your chance of influencing someone is close to zero. Your effort to be complete has achieved the opposite of your intention and you have created *active disengagement*.

Treat language as if it has a power-to-weight ratio, where every word has a weight attached. If it doesn't bring more power, then it's a dead weight and don't use it.

The other mistake I made as a recently reformed academic was using jargon that was specific to my industry. When you use jargon, your audience will have one of two responses to you, neither of which is helpful for your chances of influencing them.

The first possibility is that they will feel annoyed you've used a term without realizing it's irrelevant to them. In this case, the person will unconsciously assume you lack self-awareness. The second possibility is that they will feel insecure because they think they should know something that they don't. In this case, they feel disempowered.

Either way, you've put them in the wrong state of mind. They should feel better after hearing you, not worse. In either case, you have associated a negative feeling (annoyance or disempowerment) with your presence. Hardly a good idea if you want to influence them.

So how do you solve each of these succinctness issues? The first way is to improve readability by shortening your sentence and word length. This means choosing short common words over longer less common words, even if you have a good vocabulary. For example, use 'chance' instead of 'opportunity' and 'use' instead of 'utilize'.

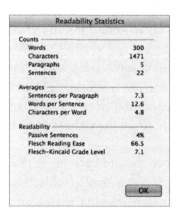

Use Readability Statistics to test whether you have done this well. Most word processing software, including Microsoft Word, has this tool. Find it by searching for Readability Statistics under the Help menu.

Don't get distracted by passive sentences and the Flesch-Kincaid

Grade level – the Flesch Reading Ease score is the only measure to care about when it comes to pitching. Unless you're writing for an academic journal, the Flesch Reading Ease score should be greater than 60. If it's not, the sentence and word length will interfere with people's ability to understand what you are saying, and therefore their ability to decide to say 'yes' to you. This is particularly important when writing proposals. However, it's almost as important when expressing ideas verbally.

The second succinctness solution is choosing to create curiosity over completeness. There are more than a hundred elements of pitching I could have written about, but by mentioning so many tools, I would have done you a great disservice. At best, you would have the illusion of knowing a lot about pitching, and, at worst, you would feel overwhelmed.

By focusing on only four aspects of pitching and four features within each aspect, you are far more likely to pick up and use the tools in this book. Similarly, you must exercise restraint in your pitches, particularly if, as I am, you are talking about a subject you are passionate about.

An incantation I've occasionally had my less succinct clients recite before they pitch is, "May my passion find its voice in the enthusiasm of my tone, not the volume of my words."

Rather than think, "I must say this because otherwise I might leave out something critical," think, "I must say only what is necessary to move this conversation to the next conversation."

Completeness kills curiosity. Less curiosity leads to less of an emotional response. Less of an emotional response means less chance of hearing 'yes'.

Instead of trying to say everything, make bold claims. Don't substantiate them all – just know that you can, when the time is right. Create tantalizing sentences such as, "This is just one of the future new business opportunities for our product." That way, your audience will be drawn in to want to ask you, "What are the other ones?"

Remember that your best chance of getting to say everything you want is not by trying to say it all at once, but by only saying enough for your audience to want to invite you back for another conversation. By saying less upfront, you gain the invitation to say more later. By saying too much upfront, you gain the right to forever hold your peace.

Finally, filtering your jargon is easier than you think. It's a matter of simply making sure you test your message on people from outside your field. If you're an engineer, have a biologist listen to your pitch, if you're a software architect, get someone from customer services, or if you work in the construction sector, try someone from retail. Or test your message on your spouse or children – anyone who is not familiar with the language of your industry.

Before you test the message, tell them what you're testing for. Ask them specifically to tell you what jargon, if any, has made its way into your pitch. This is a critical step to avoid placing someone in a situation where they either feel affronted you've used words they don't understand or insecure that they don't know something that maybe they should know.

Just as the single word 'only' has the power to turn a 'no' into a 'yes', a single word of jargon can turn a 'yes' into a 'no'.

## Questions

- How can you use framing to have conversations you've been avoiding to date?

- How can you use framing so that bolder moves seem less scary and more reasonable?

- What metaphors can you use to powerfully influence someone else's thinking and shorten the time it takes to explain unfamiliar concepts?

- Who can you use to filter jargon in your pitch?

- Do you test your pitches to see how they rate on the Flesch Reading Ease scale? If not, do so with your latest one and find out how it rates.

- Have you been guilty of the spray and pray approach to pitching? What change will you make to ensure you treat language as having a power-to-weight ratio?

CHAPTER 16

# Story

"Stories are how we think ... how we make decisions, how we justify our decisions, how we persuade others, how we understand our place in the world ... Stories are how we are wired ... To the human brain, imagined experiences are processed the same as real experiences. Stories create genuine emotions, presence (the sense of being somewhere), and behavioral responses."

– Pamela Rutledge, The Psychological Power of Storytelling, *Psychology Today*, 16 January 2011.

There are no question marks over the power of story, there are only question marks over how we apply story correctly in a commercial context. This section is about how to do that.

One of the reasons step-by-step guides on pitching fail is that they don't show you how to weave story into your pitch. It's easy to do a section on competitor analysis, another on market validation and another on the problem you solve, until you feel you have something that seems complete.

## Inspire not inform

At an informational level, such an approach may be complete, but at an inspirational level, such an approach hasn't even started. Believing that you can pitch effectively because you've picked up Guy Kawasaki's 10/20/30 rule of PowerPoint from his book *The Art of the Start* is like believing that because you have picked up a hammer, you can build a house.

One story changed the world.

In each case, what you have is a useful tool, combined with no skills for using it. How you use these tools relies a lot on your skills as a storyteller. You probably already knew that. Your question is more likely to be, how do you weave story into a commercial pitch? Let's have a story about how to use story to show you how.

It was 4 January 2015, and I'd just met Ollie, a computer science and electronics expert and genius inventor. In the tradition of Richard Pearce, Bruce Farr and John Britton, Ollie is a transport innovator. He had a genius invention that could decongest any city of traffic, was carbon neutral and cost a fraction of what it takes to develop road infrastructure. If Ollie's technology worked, it would change the world.

But that was part of Ollie's problem. What he'd invented sounded too fantastical, outlandish and futuristic for others to believe in. They saw it as high risk. None of them wanted to be the fool who had failed to see some vital showstopper and backed an idea that in hindsight turned out to be harebrained.

That fear of high risk is why less exciting ideas tend to get funding, but more game-changing ones don't. The more game changing the idea, the more the psychology of human decision making assumes the idea to be high risk. It's as if we equate high return with high risk inextricably, not believing for a moment that high reward could be coupled with anything other than high risk. It doesn't have to be this way, but it's worth understanding what you are up against if your idea is more game changing, so you can skew the odds back in your favor.

To get Ollie close to realizing his dream to commercialize his technology after 10 years of wandering in the wilderness, it was clear that we had to de-risk his proposition in the eyes of investors. And the technique we were going to use to do this was story.

To change the way that people perceived Ollie and his invention, we had to change, or rather correctly align, the investor's perception of the status quo. We had to redefine the status quo as one of change, not one where cars dominated and would always dominate.

I did some research into the history of transport and found the information to lay the cornerstone of our story. I was searching for the times when the fundamental riptide moments in transport occurred throughout history, how regularly they occurred and whether the onset of these riptide transport movements could be predicted.

If they did occur regularly and were therefore predictable, then we could show, using story, that Ollie's technology was simply the logical progression of a trend, not a harebrained disruptive idea out of the blue.

Within a month, we had totally reconfigured Ollie's story. Here's how we wove the resulting story into Ollie's pitch.

"In 1820, transport was turned on its head with the advent of the steel locomotive engine. This transformed the way that goods were transported between cities and laid the foundation of the industrial revolution. One hundred years later, in the 1920s, the mass production of the automobile again turned urban transport on its head and paved the way for the reconfiguration of large cities across the globe.

"One hundred years later, in 2020, a third riptide moment in transport evolution is before us in the form of Personal Rapid Transport (PRT), a form of transport that will again reconfigure urban cities no less substantially than the steel locomotive train or the mass production of the automobile.

"Now what's interesting is that not only do these riptide moments in transport happen, not only do they happen predictably at frequencies of around every hundred years, but more importantly the onset of these revolutions is predictable too.

"If we look to the decade preceding the 1820s, evidence abounded that the steel locomotive train would come into being. If we look at the decade preceding 1920, the technology that paved the way for the mass production of the automobile was already in place.

"And similarly, a hundred years later, we're in the decade preceding the 2020s, and right now, we again find that the technological underpinnings for the next transport revolution, which is PRT, are already in place. This will have no less significant effect on the history of transport globally, and will make those who see this future coming the owners of the future, as history has shown us to be the case."

There were many other details to the work that Ollie and I

did together. But it relied strongly on one key component – story. Because of the story, the next time that he pitched, he didn't get laughed at. He didn't get doubters. Nor did anyone say, "This sounds like something out of the Jetsons." Something different happened.

Within 48 hours, the person who heard his pitch cancelled Ollie's scheduled second round meeting and instead asked that he fly to India to give his second pitch directly to India's transport minister. Now bear in mind *this never happens*. Meeting with a government minister in India is like meeting with the Queen of England. They are the senior leaders of a country larger than the population of Europe, Russia, the United States and Canada combined, and are surrounded by entourages.

Because of the focus of his pitch, when Ollie pitched to India's transport minister, he was again well received. And within 48 hours of that pitch a media release announced that India's transport direction had changed to incorporate PRT.

At the time of writing, because he is bidding for government funding, Ollie's technology still needs to go through a tender process. We don't know the outcome of this process, nor can we speculate on his likelihood of winning.

However, in the worst-case scenario, Ollie has changed the world for the better. In the best-case scenario, not only has he changed the transport direction of the second-most-populated country on earth, but the initial bid is worth over US$600 million just to build a trial 70 km system in the outskirts of New Delhi.

But even this is not the real prize. If that trial is successful, then PRT technology could become a cornerstone technology for India's smart-city build. And India is planning to build over 200 smart cities, all of which have the capacity to run a network much bigger than the trial one, which has a build start date of just months away. The figures, the impact and the size of this win are mind-blowingly huge.

Ollie's story is one of how a single pitch changed the world. That single pitch changed the world through a single story told well.

In my spare time one evening, I looked through the winning pitch decks of companies that had received Series-B funding. Every winning pitch deck included a story. One of the pitch decks was for

LinkedIn. Theirs was a story of the exploding power of the online network.

In our third-round capital raise at Helix8, I used a story technique as well. My story was about how around the world, researchers were being thwarted in their quest to make advancements into treatments for illnesses that impacted either our lives personally or the life of a loved friend or family member. This included illnesses such as breast cancer, diabetes and rheumatoid arthritis.

These molecular biology researchers were being thwarted because the technology they used required them not only to be a molecular biologist, but also a computer scientist.

Our vision was a world where every molecular biologist could use a simple tool as easily as we use email today to accelerate the speed at which they conducted disease research, leading to twice the number of research outcomes in the same amount of time.

Our story presented the dark times where the molecular biologist was required to be a computer scientist in addition to their core work. This problem painted us as the heroes charging in on the white horse to relieve them of this tyranny.

Today, our software, together with the software programs copied from ours, has changed the lives of how more than 100,000 molecular biologists around the planet currently conducting disease research. They can now carry out their research at more than twice the speed and none of them need to be computer scientists.

Not only did the story inspire others and give us our next round of capital, but by creating a vivid image in the unconscious, it also inspired our team to feel duty bound to bring it to pass.

Truly, we don't tell stories so much as stories tell us. Story is the currency of emotional engagement. Our dream was expressed in our story. Our story became a reality.

By now you have probably realized a secret short-cut. If you use the three-part structure you picked up in Chapter 14: Structure exactly as you read it, you will be able to overlay your story, using rhetorical devices, at the same time.

Without story, your pitch will build a compelling case. With story, your pitch will win.

# Questions

- What type of story is yours – one of salvation, or new hope, or one that illustrates a theme of which you are the logical continuation?

- How can you make your story personal as we did by referring to diseases suffered by people cared about by those we pitched to?

- What storytelling devices can you use? (We borrowed the 100 years later device from Martin Luther King's 'I had a dream' speech.)

- What inspired you to do what you do in the first place?

- How can you succinctly capture the emotional essence of that inspiration in a way that inspires other people to see the world as you see it?

# Time to implement

Just to remind you, here's a summary of the power of pitching.

1. Pitching is *the* most important skill in business.

2. Pitching is *the* most important life skill you have not yet learned.

3. This book synthesizes the four parts of pitching into one simple practical form so you can be successful in your quest to lead the world to a better future.

4. The tools in this book can be learned by any committed person, including you.

5. The 16 elements of the pitch in this book are *the* essential elements of pitching. Anything else you do is non-essential. But ignore any of these elements and you will cripple your chance of winning a pitch.

6. Pitching applies to every one of these elements of business and life:

   - having someone see the value in your idea
   - enrolling someone in a cause or course
   - having someone see you in a new light
   - having someone accept your recommendation or referral
   - taking a relationship to the next level.

7. The information age creates a weight of *information*. This creates many overwhelmed people getting underwhelming success. Pitching creates a counterweight called *influence*. This causes an in-flow of people getting an overflow of success.

I wrote this book based on the above seven claims with three higher intentions in mind:

- To write a book that could change the world for the better by helping over 100,000 good people to gain great influence.

- To use stories, metaphors, questions and framing to make it almost impossible for you *not* to implement what you read.

- To include only the most useful, powerful and implementable strategies to reveal to you.

There are three things you can do immediately that will help you embed what you've just learned.

## Get support

Because of this book, there's a whole community of people who will be using pitching to change the world.

As I said right at the start, I'm forming a group for those who want to act on what they've read. I'll be available to answer your questions and share more stories, plus tell you a couple of secrets that I couldn't put in print.

The group is called Changing the World One Pitch at a Time. So if you haven't already, you can join this group right now at **fb.me/pitchtowin** and clicking the Like button.

## Let me help you

If you decide you can implement this across your life on your own, that's great. I am happy this book has served you and I look forward to reading at Changing the World One Pitch at a Time how you have used it to successfully pitch ideas that have changed the world. If you decide you need help to implement this book, that's also great. I'm happy you are being honest with yourself. I still get coaching to this day and I never intend to stop.

To give an example of the power of coaching, the technology CEOs I coach have grown their businesses a minimum of 337 percent per year through implementing the tools in this book.

To apply for coaching assistance, email me at **contact@beyondtheceiling.com**.

## Spread the word

Did this book give you something valuable you wouldn't have gained without reading it? If so, I'm sure you know other good people who deserve to have great influence.

My vision is that in this information age, a growing number of good people will create a shockwave for the better by pitching ideas that change the world. I invite you to reach out to five people and let them know you want them to buy this book.

You can practice what you have learned here, particularly about non-attachment, conviction and succinctness in your pitch as to why buying this book will be great *for them*. Can you do that? If you can, you will have already taken the first step to changing the world for the better.

# Book Daniel to speak

If you are wondering whether to engage an inspiring speaker with incredible stories, or one who gives you invaluable practical tools, you no longer need to choose – I can do both.

I speak on the following:

- How to create an engaged team in one pitch
- How to reposition yourself as a great leader in one pitch
- How to never need to beg for business in one pitch
- How to be oversubscribed for your next capital raise in one pitch
- How to gain an unfair competitive advantage in one pitch
- How to inspire a team to take total ownership in one pitch.

"Daniel is a brilliant and inspiring speaker. In fact, he's so good I've hired him to speak at our premier event for the past three years, and each time he's stolen the show. The thing with Daniel is that he is engaging, lively, authentic and thought-provoking all at the same time. His presence has that larger-than-life-ness that captures attention, and holds it in a vice-like grip that almost hurts. And, most importantly, Daniel always gives people something practical that they can use the very next day, which means he delivers instant value. The only reason I wouldn't recommend Daniel is because once the secret gets out, he'll be booked-up years ahead."

*Simon Harvey, Business Lab*

To book Daniel to speak at your next event or conference email **contact@beyondtheceiling.com**

# Book Daniel for coaching

If want one of these three things, then contact the author in person:

## 1. To win your next pitch

How much is your next pitch worth to your business? Do you want to leave winning your next pitch to chance, or do you want Daniel to help you win it?

## 2. To exponentially grow your tech company

Do you run a tech company? If so, rollercoasters of emotions, ridiculous hours and 20 percent chance of success are not what you have to endure – but they are what you have to endure if you don't learn to pitch.

If your product or service is good for the world, you can apply to be part of a highly committed group of high-tech CEOs that Daniel is growing at a minimum of 337 percent year-on-year.

## 3. To advance your cause that is changing the world for the better

Are you a solopreneur, social entrepreneur, change-maker or business owner who is doing something to make people's lives better? If you would like to get the benefit of help with applying this book, and you're good at taking on board feedback, get in touch with me.

Email Daniel at **contact@beyondtheceiling.com**.

## About the author

Daniel Batten was a member of three teams that took technology products global. He is also proof that anyone can pitch powerfully. While seeking investment in 2003, he gave what he describes as a "shockingly bad pitch". He declared "never again." Nine months later, he was New Zealand's first CEO to secure capital from an angel investment group. While running his company, he noticed that pitching happened every day and dictated how far and fast a company or career progressed. Using his unique approach, he has had outstanding success training entrepreneurs and professionals on how to pitch.